Who
You
Know

WHO YOU KNOW

Unlocking Innovations That
Expand Students' Networks

JULIA FREELAND FISHER
WITH **DANIEL FISHER**

FOREWORD BY **CLAYTON M. CHRISTENSEN**

JB JOSSEY-BASS™
A Wiley Brand

Published by Jossey-Bass
A Wiley Brand
One Montgomery Street, Suite 1000, San Francisco, CA 94104-4594—www.josseybass.com

Jossey-Bass books and products are available through most bookstores. To contact Jossey-Bass directly call our Customer Care Department within the U.S. at 800-956-7739, outside the U.S. at 317-572-3986, or fax 317-572-4002.

Wiley also publishes its books in a variety of electronic formats and by print-on-demand. Some material included with standard print versions of this book may not be included in e-books or in print-on-demand. If this book refers to media such as a CD or DVD that is not included in the version you purchased, you may download this material at http://booksupport.wiley.com. For more information about Wiley products, visit www.wiley.com.

Library of Congress Cataloging-in-Publication Data are available

ISBN 9781119452928 (cloth), 9781119452942 (ebk), 9781119452935 (ebk)

Cover image: © kyoshino/Getty Images
Cover design: Wiley

Printed in the United States of America

FIRST EDITION

F10001873_070418

CONTENTS

FOREWORD

Clayton M. Christensen

MANAGERS AND EXECUTIVES IN EVERY INDUSTRY HUNGER FOR GROWTH. GROWTH FOR THEIR employees, growth for their bottom lines, and growth for their customers as they improve products and services over time. For a school leader the quest is the same, though much more personal. How can we create an environment that helps our students grow and fulfill their unique and enormous potential?

For over twenty years, I have studied the puzzle of growth, trying to understand where it comes from and what happens to it. During that time the theory of disruptive innovation emerged, which asserts that massive growth opportunities are available by developing simple solutions for individuals who have historically not had access to existing offerings. As disruptive innovations improve over time, entire industries and sectors are transformed.

For the past ten years, we have been applying disruptive innovation theory to our schools, and concluded that online and blended learning stand to transform teaching and learning for every single student. And although this transformation serves to disrupt the forces influencing *what* our students know, Julia insightfully points out that there is perhaps an even more powerful disruptive opportunity in our schools—one that will dramatically impact *whom* our students know. This next wave of disruption has the potential to provide new and powerful relationships to millions of students who are left behind in our schools simply because of the limits of their surroundings.

For school leaders searching for new growth opportunities for their students, Julia's work is groundbreaking. All the academic interventions and supports in the world do little to change the opportunities contained in a child's inherited network—the collection of individuals in her home and community given to her at birth. Fortunately, tools and services are emerging that can change a child's fate by giving her a chance to interact and build relationships that expand her horizons, alter her perspectives, and generate opportunities. Like all disruptive innovations, these solutions are simple applications targeting simple problems. Over time, however, they stand to upend the ways students can access and capitalize on meaningful relationships.

I have gained so many marvelous insights from my time working with Julia and watching her lead this important work. A large part of my appreciation has come as I have reflected on the "strong ties" in my own life. Growing up on the wrong side of the tracks in Salt Lake City, I was fortunate to have been born to parents who had both attended college—an outright anomaly in my community. My mother wrote and spoke about politics and important issues in our home, and my father ran for the Utah state legislature despite his simple background as a grocery store manager. Together, my parents and community gave me a vision that I could be someone important in this world and have an impact—which is something every young person deserves, and every school should aim to deliver.

Over the past twenty years as an educator, manager, and father, I've realized that it's not professional accolades that will be the measure of my life. Instead, what will matter most is how I helped individual people become better. This book suggests a structure of school that would allow more individuals—even those that we don't think of as part of our traditional education system—to mentor, support, and inspire young people. In that vein, Julia's research and vision are indispensable to building a world in which individuals—even those from wildly different backgrounds—can help one another.

I'm indebted to Julia for helping me see how disruptive innovation can play a part in providing diverse, meaningful, and enduring relationships for our students. Academic supports may last for a time, but the impact of relationships can bless a student's life forever. How can schools take advantage of this monumental opportunity? *Who You Know* points the way forward.

WHO
YOU
KNOW

INTRODUCTION

WHO YOU KNOW MATTERS. WE CAN ALL THINK BACK TO A TIME WHEN A PERSONAL connection opened a new door to opportunity—or pushed us over the finish line. And we can all recall instances when somebody else, by virtue of his relationships, came out ahead of us.

Put simply, oftentimes opportunity is social. Social ties inherently shape our man-made systems. Whom you know turns out to matter across all sorts of industries and institutions: it matters if you're an entrepreneur trying to raise capital, an investor choosing among stocks, a patient seeking out health care, or a graduate in search of a job.[1] In fact, over *half* of all job placements result from a personal connection.[2]

But even with so much success hinging on our connections, one of our most central institutions almost entirely ignores the question of whom we know: our schools.

This is not to say that schools are by any means *anti*social environments. Seminal architects of our American education system such as John Dewey imagined modern education as a fundamentally social endeavor. Dewey believed that each school ought to function as an "embryonic community life." He insisted that schools should train children how to behave in society by inducting them into a "little community" of their peers.

Dewey's vision resonates with much of society's concept of what makes school, school. Today, parents rank acquiring social and communication skills among their top priorities for their children, next to study habits, critical thinking, and college preparation.[3]

But Dewey envisioned a *little*—even *embryonic*—school community. Which is exactly, by and large, what our schools have become. At best, schools today function as highly self-contained communities that may manage—between teaching skills and content and doing their best to ensure that students are safe and cared for—to impart social norms in their students. The implicit hope, then, is that by appropriately socializing children at a young age, schools prepare them to eventually hatch into the real world ready to interact.

As a result, by their very design, schools limit their students' access to people beyond their embryonic community. They are not built to nurture the health of their students' networks or to connect students in predictable and effective ways beyond their immediate constellation of teachers, family, and peers. With an eye toward socialization and establishing a tight-knit community, we have turned schools inside, rather than out.

In turn, many students leave school with a network that resembles the one they inherited at birth. Students who go on to college may buck this trend if they manage to attend an institution that connects them with new peers, professors, and alumni career networks. However, a large proportion of low-income students who could benefit *most* from these new connections never make it to college, and a large percentage of those who do attend fail to graduate.

Ignoring whom students know should be cause for concern for anyone working to close widening opportunity gaps. Relationships help young people get by and get ahead. Networks offer academic, emotional, and financial supports, as well as critical information and endorsements that open doors to new interests, opportunities, and even careers.

Take the great John Dewey himself: like many of today's millennials, after graduating college Dewey spent the summer wondering what to do next. With few prospects, he wrangled a favor from his cousin, Affia Wilson. Wilson, the principal of the local high school in Oil City, Pennsylvania, hired him to teach. For all the promise he would later realize as a seminal leader, it was a relationship—rather than his innate abilities alone—that landed Dewey his first job in a lifelong career in education.

Why Are We Ignoring Students' Networks?

The tendency of our K–12 education system to ignore students' networks is hardly surprising if we consider just how busy schools are kept trying to accomplish other things. In recent years, schools have come under enormous pressure to demonstrate their ability to drive up test scores—an effort that has proven persistently challenging. When President George W. Bush rolled out his flagship 2001 No Child Left Behind Education Act, his vision was seemingly simple: by measuring student outcomes and requiring that chronically underperforming schools improve, we could successfully close stubborn racial and socioeconomic achievement gaps by 2014.

What students knew—or didn't know—sat at the core of this vision. When Bush signed the bill, he insisted that schools needed to focus on the basics. "Every school has a job to do," he said. "And that's to teach the basics and teach them well. If we want to make sure no child is left behind, every child must learn to read. And every child must learn to add and subtract."[4]

The federal law, in other words, squarely focused on nailing basic proficiency in literacy and numeracy. Years later, despite modest improvement—and a few pockets of great success—schools are still scrambling to meet this charge, particularly those serving high-poverty and minority populations. Meanwhile, political battles wage over precisely what standards states should aim to meet and the best methods of teaching to get us there. In short, schools and society remain intently focused on *what* students know.

But this focus suffers from a critical blind spot. With everyone talking about what our students do and don't know, no one is talking about whom students know. Children's networks—their reservoir of social capital and ability to bank on that capital for support, advice, or opportunities down the line—remains largely determined by random luck: the luck of where children are born, whom their parents know, and whom they happen to end up sitting next to in class.

Put simply, the term *social capital* describes the benefits that people can accrue by virtue of their relationships or membership in social networks or other social structures.[5] This book will explore young people's access to relationships that might help them further their potential and their goals, as those goals emerge and shift over time. Of course, students may involve themselves in relationships or social networks that do little to help them advance in a positive direction. The goal of our education system, however, should be to arm all young people with networks that can reliably expand access to support, guidance, new opportunities, and positive life outcomes.

For decades, researchers have studied the basic principle that whom you know—both your strong connections and even your mere acquaintances—can matter quite a bit in lifelong success or failure. The strength of our networks even appears to predict our longevity.[6] So why, then, do our schools not heed their importance?

At first glance, it's easy to blame the recent high-stakes nature of accountability and testing focused narrowly on what students know. But other cultural factors dating much further back than No Child Left Behind discourage schools from nurturing students' networks.

The very concepts of childhood and young adulthood can help to explain our aversion to expanding young people's networks. For centuries, we've treated childhood as a sacred period of innocence and fragility during which young people ought to be sheltered and protected, and only gradually exposed to the ways of the world. As Phillip Aries, famed French historian of childhood and family, put it, for much of history children were alternately thought of as "charming toys" or "fragile creatures of God who needed to be safeguarded and reformed."[7] Early on, coddling or reforming children fell to the family. Later, as compulsory schooling spread through Western Europe and North America at the turn of the twentieth century, the responsibility to protect children shifted gradually to educators as well. Society delegated child rearing alternately to families and schools and then shut the door behind them.[8]

This impulse to protect children is more formalized than ever in our school systems and policies. In the wake of high-profile school shootings and growing reams of computer-based student data, over the past decade federal and state legislators have continued to ratchet up school safety regulations and student privacy laws.

Protecting children, in and of itself, is of course a very good thing. Children *are* more vulnerable to abuse. Their healthy development depends on ensuring that the adults charged with their care do right by that responsibility. But an outgrowth of these cultural norms is also a willful isolation of children. In the name of safety, we risk cutting off children's chances to expand their horizons and their networks.

This isolation comes at a particularly high cost for those children who lack sufficient support networks at home, or whose networks offer limited inroads to social mobility later on when they enter the labor market. What happens beyond school buildings exacerbates these effects. As income inequality increases, it produces unequal childhoods along a variety of dimensions—for example, access to schools, health care, and extracurricular opportunities. Families from different sides of the tracks are living in increasing isolation from one another. Neighborhoods themselves have regressed back to higher levels of socioeconomic segregation. And exposure to poor neighborhoods also still falls disproportionately along racial lines.[9]

Trends like these call into question our school system's ability to function as society's great equalizer. If a child's "embryonic community" is itself a reflection of his immediate neighborhood, children's networks are systematically cut off from peers and adults hailing from different socio-economic and cultural backgrounds and limited to the regions where they live. This leads to stark gaps in both the volume and diversity of young people's networks.

To this day, neighborhoods and schools by and large hold a monopoly on children's networks. Unsurprisingly, this costs poor children the most. On average, children from low-income families have measurably smaller networks along some dimensions and are much less likely to know adults working in high-paying professions.

The Potential to Disrupt Opportunity Gaps

Against this backdrop, however, the education system is undergoing major shifts.

As society grapples with the economic and political harms of growing inequality, the role of schools themselves is changing. With the rapid rise of technology, delivering academic content—once a key value proposition of traditional classrooms—is becoming commoditized. No longer must a teacher stand at the front of a class for students to access content. Students can now access a lecture, project, or assessment from a mobile phone anywhere in their home, neighborhood, or school building.

At the same time, schools are increasingly trying to ensure that they are modernizing their approaches to meet the demands of a changing economy. Many are turning to real-world projects and assessments. These mark an effort to make learning more relevant and engaging while instilling "twenty-first-century skills"—such as collaboration and critical thinking—that employers demand.

And as a college degree becomes a must-have in the modern economy, education reformers are finding that social supports are a critical ingredient to getting students into and through college.

In light of these shifts, schools are now well positioned to prioritize not merely what students know but also whom they know. And as technology improves, schools for the first time have tools that make investing in students' social capital viable on a strict budget. These forces stand to allow schools to begin to further chip away at stark divisions that have hampered schools' ability to deliver on equal opportunity for students rich and poor, white and minority, well-connected and isolated.

One of the critical forces underlying these shifts is disruptive innovation. Disruption is a market phenomenon that expands access to goods and services that are otherwise too expensive, centralized, and out of reach to many. Harvard Business School professor Clayton Christensen developed the theory of disruptive innovation in the 1980s and 1990s when he began to notice that wildly successful companies and entire industries would suddenly give way to new competitors that were offering seemingly rudimentary products and services. Christensen's research bucked the traditional wisdom that blamed senior management at these struggling firms. Instead, he theorized that new innovations displaced incumbents because they effectively competed on new dimensions such as affordability and accessibility. He coined this phenomenon *disruptive innovation.*

Decades later, the nonprofit Clayton Christensen Institute, where Julia has worked for over five years, is bringing these theories to bear on the public sector. The Institute's research on innovation shows that improving products and services at a pace that satisfies customers is actually rarely a problem. Most institutions want to keep improving what they do—and generally they are quite good at doing just that.

Our education system is no different.

As Michael Horn, Curtis Johnson, and Clay Christensen pointed out in their groundbreaking work, *Disrupting Class,* contrary to widespread perception, on average, public schools have a steady record of improving on the metrics by which they are judged, just like the other organizations we've studied. What our studies of innovation show, however, is that disruptive innovations almost always trip up well-managed, improving companies because the definitions and trajectories of improvement change. What were valuable improvements before the disruption now are less relevant, and dimensions of the product that had been unimportant become highly valued.

Today, our education system focuses the majority of its energy on getting better and better at delivering and measuring what students know. The system in turn vastly undervalues children and young adults' access to meaningful networks, which leads to stark gaps in access to mentors, supportive adults, industry experts, and diverse peer groups. As a result, advantageous connections, formal and informal mentors, peer networks, and exposure to professions and professionals reside in exclusive networks that children access by sheer luck of the draw.

It bears noting that schools are not *causing* these gaps. Rather, by design they do little to resolve them. Children's immediate community—not merely their school—holds a monopoly on their network. Schools, however, institutionalize this monopoly by closing rather than opening their doors to people beyond that embryonic community.

But disruptive innovations are beginning to emerge that will reshape how we connect students to coaches, mentors, experts, and peers. These innovations stand to radically expand students' access to social capital down the line. Online coaching, mentoring, and tutoring programs are beginning to penetrate schools and homes. Online peer networks—sometimes seen merely as social networks for sharing silly photos or vapid life updates—are increasingly used to connect students to additional resources otherwise out of reach.

And inside classrooms themselves, students are starting to interact with real-life experts from a wealth of industries using video chats and social learning platforms. Finally, new human capital management systems—modeled on platforms that align new channels of supply and demand, such as Uber and eBay—are beginning to tap into a latent supply of local experts, community members, and supportive adults who can slot into schools. In light of these innovations, how students connect—to one another, to their teachers, and to new adult mentors, guides, and role models—stands to shift dramatically in the coming decades. These innovations in turn stand to disrupt the limitations ingrained in all students' inherited networks.

These developments are truly remarkable if we consider how unimaginable they were only a few decades ago. Historically, limited communications and transportation infrastructure made it difficult—if not logistically impossible—for schools to function as networking hubs, rather than as Dewey's embryonic communities. As a result, students' access to networks has remained strictly bound by time and space.

Tight-knit school communities were not the only ones subject to these strict limitations. For decades, large-scale mentoring efforts like Big Brothers Big Sisters have required specific time commitments when mentors can meet in person with mentees—a requirement that on the one hand vastly limits its ability to recruit volunteers and on the other makes mentorship a strictly local phenomenon. This poses challenges to quality and scale—quality because the costs of recruiting and retaining first-rate nonteacher volunteers are high, and scale because geographic and time limitations cap the number of feasible relationships and interactions at the programs' disposal. As a result, one in three children will grow up without a mentor.

Innovating toward Relationships

With the rise of technology, however, new tools and networking models stand to break these limitations. Technology can dramatically expand young people's access to and ability to maintain relationships with new and diverse adults and peers. Online communication tools can reach beyond geographic boundaries to forge new connections, as well as strengthen and better coordinate existing networks in their immediate communities.

All sorts of familiar tools have been steadily improving over the past decades, such as email, texting, and video chatting. Even newer technologies such as matching algorithms, virtual reality, and artificial intelligence have emerged. As a result, students will be able to connect and form relationships more often and with more supportive adults and peers than ever before.

In case this sounds like a bleak future mediated by screens, fear not. These opportunities will also emerge through new school designs that facilitate *in-person* relationships more deliberately and frequently. Disruptive innovations, in other words, will not just digitize students' social lives. Rather, innovations are starting to orchestrate a whole new choreography of care and opportunity across school communities, both face-to-face and online.

This networked model of education will not come about merely from the use of existing social networking tools. Popular platforms, such as Facebook and LinkedIn, tend to simply amplify users' offline networks and tendencies, rather than forging new, different, or expanded networks. Instead, new tools that connect students are being curated and designed in an effort to expand student networks to new corners of their communities and the globe. These new relationships and networks can in turn make valuable headway in evening the playing field of students' opportunities and expanding their sense of what is possible.

For example, consider Zachary, a Jamaican-born teen, who moved to the US with his family when he was sixteen years old. His high school in New York matched students with mentors using iMentor, an organization that provides a platform and curriculum that blends virtual and face-to-face mentoring. Zachary was paired with Eric, a senior lawyer with the General Counsel Division of Credit Suisse. The two collaborated on the iMentor curriculum through weekly email exchanges and in-person meetings. Eric helped Zachary not only to study for the SAT but also to build his resume, seek out summer enrichment experiences, and research college opportunities beyond his radar. In spring 2013, Zachary was accepted to his top-choice school, the Massachusetts Institute of Technology.[10]

We all have heard inspiring stories like these. What's unique about Zachary's story is not that a helpful adult could get him one step closer to college or that mentorship programs could successfully forge relationships across class and race lines. Crucially, it's the model that underlies this relationship that marks important innovation: the iMentor model leverages technology to make relationships like Zachary and Eric's far more tenable and scalable in terms of both cost and geography. The two could keep in touch with far more regularity between in-person meetings, and Eric could track Zachary's progress against his goals in a more reliable way.

At the same time, innovations are starting to expand students' connections long before the college application gauntlet. In her elementary school classroom in the small rural town of Royse City, Texas, teacher Kelly Margot decided to break out of the four walls of her science class. She used a tool called Nepris, which offers access to industry experts over video. Margot ported a neurologist into her classroom during a lesson on the human brain. For some students, the brief connection fueled new academic interests. "[The next day] a student came in fired up about his next research idea over cures for neurological issues. The expert told the kids what happens in the brain that causes autism. This kid wants to know what is being done to fix it," Margot said. For other students, Margot witnessed a different spark ignite. Her students who had not traveled beyond the Texas border were thrilled by the chance to see the New York City skyline outside the neurologist's office.[11]

The power of technology tools, in other words, is not to merely digitize existing relationships between young people and adults. Instead, these tools stand to bust through the ceiling that geography and time have long held over networks. In turn, new tools are beginning to both strengthen students' connections and broaden their horizons.

In light of these possibilities, we are witnessing an emerging market of technology-enabled platforms and school models designed to connect students in new ways. These tools have the potential to fundamentally disrupt our traditional school models that close off, rather than open up, students' networks. And if these innovations grow in the right way, we will not only manage to scale critical supports that can transform students' short-term accomplishments. We will also scale students' access to an array of relationships that can lend valuable perspective, supports, and opportunities in the longer term.

Many in education may hear this as yet another job being piled on top of already cash-strapped and busy schools. Given persistent academic achievement gaps, mightn't it be prudent to just heed Bush's vision and go back to basics? Ought schools really aim to do even *more*, when nailing basic literacy and numeracy remains insurmountable for so many?

Yes, they should. Growing students' networks, it turns out, could prove instrumental in solving chronic challenges that our education system has struggled with in the past. For example, we know that poverty erects barriers to learning from a young age. But we don't invest in the very social supports that could predictably combat those detrimental effects of poverty on children's healthy development. We often lament the human capital crisis in K–12 education by citing shortages of high-quality teachers. In reality, however, the world offers an abundance of human capital across all sorts of industries and neighborhoods. We just haven't designed a school system or the right tools to tap into that huge reserve. Similarly, we focus relentlessly on closing the achievement gap to enhance social mobility, yet we systematically ignore gaps in poor and minority students' access to power and relationships that could engender such mobility. We consider the importance of "real-world" relevance in education, but fail to pursue instructional models that could authentically connect what happens inside classrooms with the wide range of industries in the real world.

These structural impediments threaten schools' ability to address achievement and opportunity gaps alike. We can start to overcome these perennial obstacles by investing in relationships. From there, we can reimagine school as a networking hub, rather than as an embryonic community.

The Purpose of This Book

Charting human relationships is a vast and, at times, mysterious endeavor. Given the complexity of this topic and the various paths this book could have taken, we want to clarify what this book is—and what it is not.

This book is primarily about the structures, tools, and institutional designs that could start to double down on relationships *inside* school and take the chance out of students' chance encounters *beyond* school. We consider how relationships could become embedded in every aspect of a student's K–12 experience not only to enrich learning but also to nurture connecting. These connections range from students' strongest-tie relationships with caretakers to their diverse weak-tie networks beyond their immediate community.

This is *not* a book about higher education. Oftentimes when we talk about this topic, people think of the "network" that college students enjoy. Many readers may picture college as a pivotal moment when, by design, students fly the proverbial nest and expand their relationships beyond the network and neighborhood they inherited at birth.

Treating college as the gateway to new networks, however, leaves too many students out of the opportunity equation. By the time a student reaches eighteen, her network has already determined all sorts of aspects of her educational trajectory—from her identity to her career ambitions, from her access to extracurricular activities to her understanding of the knowledge economy and the steps it takes to make it to and through postsecondary education. Not to mention that those students who might benefit *most* from deeper, stronger, and more diverse relationships are often those least likely to make it to, much less through, college. Therefore, part of the premise of this book is that we can't rely solely on colleges to function as the primary institutions responsible for expanding student networks. Instead, we believe that efforts to nurture students' networks must begin far earlier, as a key component of our K–12 schools' design. That said, we will discuss how some schools are continuing to invest in students' networks into and through college in an effort to address persistent opportunity gaps.

This is also *not* a book about relationship science or the politics of networks. Although we borrow heavily from sociology and psychology research, we do not claim to be experts in the science of how relationships or identities form and change over time. Nor do we endeavor to be experts in the transmission of culture through relationships, how racial or ethnic discrimination and bias affect and limit networks, or the ways in which political dynamics have over time shaped neighborhoods and networks. These topics are critically important in their own right. They all merit deeper, further research beyond this book. Throughout, we suggest a number of researchers who delve into the interpersonal, cultural, and political facets of relationships.

We focus most on how new *structures* of schools and tools could begin to free up time, space, and resources to invest more heavily in students' networks inside and beyond school. Throughout, we explore the enormous potential that technology offers to radically expand students' access to new networks, particularly those students from low-income, rural, or urban settings whose access to networks has historically limited their access to supports and opportunities. We also offer other theories of innovation that explain how schools could better offer crucial in-person care and support to their students who need it most.

Chapter 1 takes stock of the role that relationships play in today's opportunity equation. The chapter details the current state of meritocracy in America and discusses widening gaps in children's access to opportunity. It establishes why relationships are an important but underexamined component of the opportunity equation and why schools cannot afford to ignore students' networks any longer.

Chapter 2 defines the term *social capital,* **provides a synthesis of the research on how networks form, and explores why certain sorts of relationships or "ties" offer different benefits in different circumstances.** It also introduces the concept of interdependence and modularity, a theory of innovation that predicts when and why industries function in an integrated or modular manner. Specifically, schools can learn from the wisdom that most successful enterprises tend to pursue interdependent architectures in circumstances when they need to increase performance.

Chapter 3 analyzes what schools must do when students lack sufficient care and support networks, inhibiting their opportunities to both learn and connect. In these circumstances, schools must expand their efforts to address the nonacademic barriers that impact learning and access to opportunity. The chapter takes a deep look at one program, City Connects, that is successfully integrating student supports to simultaneously strengthen connections to services in their communities and deepen teacher-student relationships.

Chapter 4 highlights the potential for emerging education technology tools to disrupt the limitations of students' inherited networks. The chapter profiles a small set of entrepreneurs leading this charge. It describes the theory of disruptive innovation and why technology tools could begin to fill gaps in students' networks where relationships are otherwise out of reach. Specifically, it explores how technology could broaden student networks along a variety of dimensions such as career exposure, college guidance, and academic encouragement and support. It also discusses the design principles such tools will need to embrace if schools hope to establish trusting ties amid diversifying and expanding student networks.

Chapter 5 ties together the previous four chapters to consider what the future of a more relationship-centered school might look like. The chapter considers examples of schools that are striving to open up additional "slots" for a variety of relationships inside and outside school. Through a deep look at the evolution of these schools, it describes the business models that will underpin a future of fundamentally more flexible approaches to learning and connecting.

Chapter 6 explores what might motivate a wide array of mentors, experts, and community members to engage with schools and students in a new, networked system. It describes the theory of "Jobs to Be Done," a model for understanding what motivates people to hire products and services to make progress in their lives. Applying this theory to the school and mentorship space, it follows that schools and tools must avoid a "build it and they will come" approach. Rather, any new school architecture that adequately addresses social capital gaps will have to design itself around the jobs to be done of students, teachers, and prospective mentors.

Chapter 7 considers how schools might start to measure student networks in meaningful ways. It offers policy frameworks and metrics that will ensure deeper investment into expanding students' social capital, and the protections and quality control measures that will need to be in place to ensure that a networked school system is at once safe, flexible, and effective.

In sum, this book charts a path forward to building an approach to K–12 education that pays far more attention to whom its students know. With this new reality in mind, we can get to work imagining schools that by their very design stretch these networks to the people and places that for young people, for decades, have remained out of reach.

Notes

1. Baker, W. E. (2000). *Achieving success through social capital: Tapping the hidden resources in your personal and business networks*. San Francisco, CA: Jossey-Bass; Casson, M., & Giusta, M. D. (2007). Entrepreneurship and social capital: Analysing the impact of social networks on entrepreneurial activity from a rational action perspective. *International Small Business Journal, 25*(3), 220–244. doi:10.1177/0266242607076524; Cohen, L., Frazzini, A., & Malloy, C. (2010). Sell-side school ties. *Journal of Finance, 65*(4), 1409–1437. Retrieved from http://www.nber.org/papers/w13973; Lin, N. (1999). Building a network theory of social capital. *Connections, 22*(1), 28–51. Retrieved from http://www.insna.org/PDF/Connections/v22/1999_I-1-4.pdf; Perry, M., Williams, R. L., Wallerstein, N., & Waitzkin, H. (2008). Social capital and health care experiences among low-income individuals. *American Journal of Public Health, 98*(2), 330–336. doi:10.2105/AJPH.2006.086306

2. Many studies demonstrate the centrality of social networks in job hunting. Aaron Smith's 2015 Pew survey found that 55 percent of respondents used information from acquaintances or friends-of-friends, 63 percent used professional or network connections, and 66 percent used connections from close friends or family. The 1981–82 National Longitudinal Survey of Youth showed that 87 percent of then-employed and 85 percent of then-unemployed workers used friends and relatives as sources of information, among other methods (Holzer, 1987). Other research has focused on job acquisition through networks. A 1956 survey of textile workers in a New England town found that 62 percent of respondents "had found out about and applied to their first job through a social contact" (Myers & Shultz, 1977). Ornstein (1971) surveyed a randomized sample of sixteen hundred American men, with 55.8 percent of whites and 58.9 percent of blacks noting that they used "personal" means to get their first job. A few years later, Lin, Ensel, and Vaughn (1981) analyzed survey data from residents of the Albany, New York, metropolitan area and found that 59 percent of respondents landed their current job using personal contacts. And a 1995 study of male white-collar workers in a Boston suburb showed that 56 percent of respondents used personal connections in acquiring their current job (Granovetter, 1995).

   Granovetter, M. (1995). *Getting a job: A study of contacts and careers*. Chicago, IL: University of Chicago Press; Holzer, H. J. (1987). Job search by employed and unemployed youth. *ILR Review, 40*(4), 601–611. doi:10.1177/001979398704000411; Lin, N., Ensel, W. M., & Vaughn, J. C. (1981). Social resources and strength of ties: Structural factors in occupational status attainment. *American Sociological Review, 46*, 393–405. doi:10.2307/2095260; Myers, C. A., & Shultz, G. P. (1977). The dynamics of a labor market: A study of the impact of employment changes on labor mobility, job satisfactions, and company and union policies. (n.p.): Greenwood Press; Ornstein, M. D. (1971). Entry into the American labor force. *Johns Hopkins University Center for Social Organization of Schools, 113*. Retrieved from http://files.eric.ed.gov/fulltext/ED055250.pdf; Smith, A. (2015). Searching for work in the digital era. Retrieved from http://www.pewinternet.org/2015/11/19/searching-for-work-in-the-digital-era

3. Zeehandelaar, D., & Winkler, A. M. (2013). What parents want: Education preferences and trade-offs. Retrieved from https://edexcellence.net/publications/what-parents-want.html

4. The White House, Office of the Press Secretary. (2002). President signs landmark No Child Left Behind Education bill [Press release]. Retrieved from http://georgewbush-whitehouse.archives.gov/news/releases/2002/01/20020108-1.html

5. Portes, A. (1998). Social capital: Its origins and applications in modern sociology. *Annual Review of Sociology, 24*(1), 1–24. doi:10.1146/annurev.soc.24.1.1

6. Pinker, S. (2014). *The village effect: How face-to-face contact can make us healthier and happier.* Toronto, Canada: Random House Canada.

7. Aries, P. (1962). *Centuries of childhood* (p. 133). London, UK: Jonathan Cape.

8. It bears noting that racial disparities have led to divergent perceptions of "childhood" and disparate treatment of children from different backgrounds. For example, see Martin, M. (Host). (2014, March 19). Consequences when African-American boys are seen as older [Radio program]. In C. Watson (Producer), *Tell Me More.* Washington, D.C.: NPR News. Retrieved from http://www.npr.org/2014/03/19/291405871/consequences-when-african-american-boys-are-seen-as-older

9. Reardon, S. F., Fox, L., & Townsend, J. (2015). Neighborhood income composition by household race and income, 1990–2009. *Annals of the American Academy of Political and Social Science, 660*(1), 78–97. doi:10.1177/0002716215576104

10. Richardson, C. (2013, April 26). Great people: Williamsburg Prep valedictorian Zachary Beaumont-Kelly is headed to MIT in the fall. *NY Daily News.* Retrieved from http://www.nydailynews.com/new-york/great-people-brooklyn-high-school-scholar-headed-mit-article-1.1327621

11. Carolan, J. (2016). Why VR matters especially in rural schools. *TechCrunch.* Retrieved from https://techcrunch.com/2016/09/19/why-vr-matters-especially-in-rural-schools

CHAPTER ONE

The Social Side of Opportunity
Why Relationships Matter to Meritocracy

Meritocracy's Mythical Origins

The year is 2033, and Britain is witnessing an upheaval in the face of vast inequality. A fragmented underclass wages its final revolt against the meritocracy—an economic and political system that has, for nearly a century, purported to sort people into various schools and jobs according to their talents. The merit-based machinery was originally designed to combat class divides. But it has failed to account for the uneven playing field many face, and has ended up simply reproducing a society profoundly divided between haves and have-nots.[1]

In 1958, then-fledgling sociologist Michael Young envisioned this bleak British future in his essay *The Rise of the Meritocracy*. Young intended the piece to be both a satire and a warning. At the time, he was concerned that all sorts of worthy people might inadvertently find themselves *left out* of Britain's system committed to rewarding individual merit. He worried that without equal opportunity, this system would yield unfair outcomes and create a permanent underclass. He mocked the false tidiness of this commitment to merit and dubbed it with a new name, *meritocracy*.

Young meant this made-up term to be something of a joke. The word combines the Latin verb *merere* or "earn" with the Greek suffix *cracy*— "power" or "rule" (that's bookish British humor for you!). But as use of the word spread through the second half of the twentieth century, it quite magically shed its ironic origins. Meritocracy morphed into something

17

altogether positive—and across the pond, the idea came to capture a distinctly American sentiment.

When our parents, school principals, and political leaders now talk about merit, the term is cast with a rosy hue. They celebrate a system that rewards some mix of raw talent and hard work. The vast majority of Americans subscribe to this notion. They are, in fact, one of the most likely populations in the world to favor meritocracy.[2] It has become virtually impossible to disentangle the concept of who gets what from the idea that individual capacity and effort ought to play a leading role.

As Young pointed out, however, the health of any meritocracy depends on ensuring equal access to opportunity. And in this regard, America has witnessed an ongoing struggle. If America's enthusiasm for meritocracy is alive and well, then so are Young's 1958 fears. The complexity, trade-offs, and messiness of what constitutes equal opportunity are more stark and confusing than ever.

Opportunity by the Numbers: A Tale of Two Childhoods

No institution sits more in the crossfire of meritocracy and opportunity than our schools. School is an institution responsible for providing the foundation of equal opportunity on top of which our meritocracy can stand proudly. Americans have long lauded school as society's "great equalizer."

But playing society's equalizer is no easy task. By many accounts, the contours of opportunity in America are shifting far beyond our school buildings. Our schools are being asked to level exceedingly complex—and unequal—terrain.

Drive across any US city and you'll be reminded of the vast income inequalities facing the country. The first half of the twentieth century witnessed relatively steady progress among low- and middle-wage earners. But income inequality has shot up since the 1970s. In the post-2008 Great Recession era, it has continued to grow at an astonishing clip.[3] Further, these gaps hamper economic mobility. Only half of Americans born in 1980 are economically better off than their parents, compared to 90 percent of those born a generation earlier.[4] These differences are appearing not only on Americans' bank statements but also in their zip codes. Residential segregation by income has increased since the 1980s, including in twenty-seven of the nation's thirty largest major metropolitan areas.[5]

Children, of course, are not immune to the effects of these trends. As researchers have long pointed out, families' economic and geographic circumstances have lasting impacts on gaps in children's cognitive, educational, professional, and health outcomes. This reality has grown even starker as income inequality has gotten worse. For better or for worse, schools often function as the first line of defense—and the last hope—for addressing these shifts.

Many have attempted to trace the impact that economic shifts and family circumstances have on children. For example, the Opportunity Index (a joint effort of the national campaign Opportunity Nation and the nonprofit Child Trends) compiles American state and local data to create annual composite measures on Americans' access to opportunity. Explaining the index's purpose, the organization describes two children from disparate geographies and backgrounds, John and Jane. John hails from Nassau County, New York, where the median household income is $90,634. Jane, by contrast, lives in Tarrant County, Texas, where prospects are not as bright. Tarrant County has a median income of $53,170. Its violent crime rate is more than double that of Nassau County, and its rate of enrollment in pre-K is two thirds that of Nassau.[6]

These geographic and economic conditions spell greatly different educational prospects for John and Jane. Extending the hypothetical, John attends an award-winning high school in Garden City, Long Island, which is ranked 121st nationally by *US News & World Report.* Jane lives in inner-city Fort Worth. At her high school, only 11 percent of students who qualify for free and reduced lunch are proficient in math and English.[7]

Such disparate conditions are all too familiar to those of us steeped in education reform. Economically disadvantaged children like Jane have historically had fewer developmental and early education opportunities, received less reliable health care, and enrolled in disproportionately low-performing schools.

But measuring opportunity in terms of household income or school quality doesn't paint the whole picture. John and Jane, it turns out, are competing on an even more complex playing field, one that's often masked by statistics on income and achievement. John's well-resourced childhood introduces a whole new set of inequities between him and Jane: social gaps. John and Jane possess vastly different webs of relationships that each can rely on and tap into. And if diverging income levels remain the starkest drivers of unequal childhoods, then relationships are becoming the best-hidden asset in the modern opportunity equation.[8]

Relationship Gaps: Hidden Disparity

Schools deal in the intricate webs of students' relationships every day. They interface with parents and guardians. They watch social groups form and dissolve. They forge connections between teachers and students. But because relationships are not an overt metric of school quality or educational excellence, social connections are rarely measured or talked about in their own right.

Still, data on the state of students' networks does exist—and reveals some alarming realities. In recent years, a few key statistics have emerged that paint a startling picture of divergent childhood experiences that reflect not only financial gaps but social ones.

First, neighborhood segregation is worsening as families from different income brackets are living further apart. (See Figure 1.1.) For example, Texas, where Jane lives, has seen some of the worst rates of income-based residential segregation in the country over the past thirty years. Her family's low-income status renders it disproportionately likely to live among other poor families. In fact, in the Dallas–Fort Worth–Arlington metropolitan area, residential segregation by income has gotten worse by a whopping 54 percent.[9]

These growing neighborhood gaps—by entire cities or even just block by block—inevitably change school demographics too. For example, from 2000 to 2014, the percentage of all K–12 public schools that had high proportions of poor and black or Hispanic students grew from 9 to 16 percent.[10]

Highly segregated schools leave poor minority students at both an academic disadvantage (as seen in well-known measures such as advanced coursework) and a social one. Access to college guidance provides one of the starkest cases of this divide: abysmal national guidance counselor

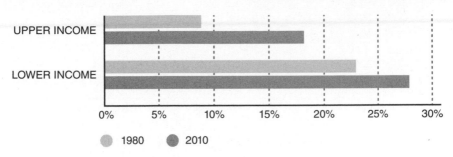

Figure 1.1 Growing Neighborhood Segregation: Percentage of Households Living among Others at Similar Income Levels

Source: Data from Pew Research Center, 2006–2010 American Community Survey and Geolytics 1980 Census data in 2000 boundaries. "The Rise of Residential Segregation by Income," Pew Research Center, Washington, DC (August 1, 2012), http://www .pewsocialtrends.org/2012/08/01/the-rise-of-residential-segregation-by-income/

ratios mean that students at many public schools spend only thirty-eight minutes per year with a counselor.[11] Those students who would stand to benefit most from high-quality, high-touch counseling end up being the least likely to receive it.[12] These gaps are even more troubling if we look at the other sorts of adult personnel cropping up on high-poverty, high-minority campuses. For example, minorities are between roughly 20 and 40 percent more likely to be one of the 1.6 million students who attend a school where there is a school law enforcement officer but no guidance counselor.[13]

School segregation is one of the most visible social gaps that education reformers have witnessed since compulsory schooling began. Gaps in access to networks, however, are cropping up well beyond school buildings. And that brings us to two more troubling data points with which schools must grapple.

Second, over the last three decades, the amount of time that college-educated parents spend with their children has dramatically increased, relative to that of their less-educated peers. John's college-educated parents have arranged their schedules around his elaborate after-school and summer commitments. They make it to every basketball game and host team dinners after big wins. His dad has even set aside Wednesday nights to do extra math prep with John for his weekly geometry quizzes.

Jane's mom does everything she can to spend high-quality time with her daughter. In fact, she's spending more time with Jane than her own

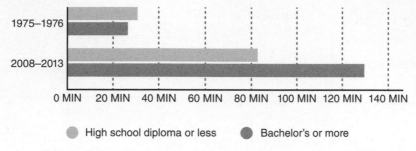

Figure 1.2 Growing Gaps in Amount of Developmental Time Children Spend with Parents Daily

Source: Data from "The Widening Education Gap in Developmental Child Care Activities in the United States, 1965–2013," by Evrim Altintas, 2016, *Journal of Marriage and Family, 78*(1), 38. doi:10.1111/jomf.12254.

mom managed to spend with her. But with competing work and family obligations, she can't hope to keep up with John's parents' level of involvement. On average, college-educated parents are spending more than four times as much developmental time with their offspring as they did three decades ago. Today, they spend more than one-and-a-half times as many developmental minutes with their children as their less-educated parent peers (see Figure 1.2).[14]

As if this difference were not enough, John's parents are able to offer him an additional social asset besides their own time: a disproportionately professionalized social network of their own. More educated parents are more likely to know more people working in the knowledge economy: on average, their social networks include at least twice as many politicians, CEOs, and professors than their peers who received a high school education or less (see Figure 1.3).[15]

If more educated parents are increasingly sharing their own time and connections with their children, they are also effectively purchasing a wider array of relationships through a bevy of out-of-school activities. This brings us to the third emerging statistic that suggests troubling relationship gaps.

Third, as income inequality has grown, children from wealthy families are enjoying a boom in enrichment spending relative to their low-income peers. John has a packed schedule of math tutoring, club basketball, and volunteering at the local YMCA. His basketball schedule involves both his high school coach and outside trainers who work with

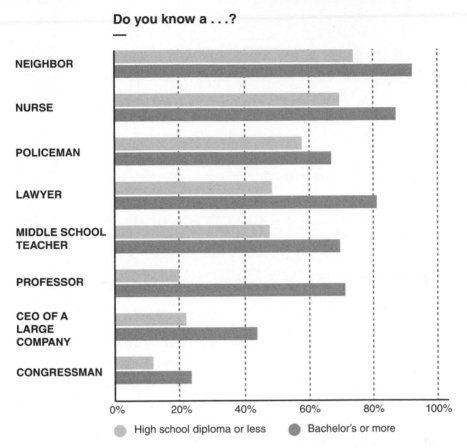

Do you know a . . . ?

Figure 1.3 Parents' Networks in the Knowledge Economy Vary by Education Level

Source: Data from Robert D. Putnam, *Our Kids: The American Dream in Crisis,* 2015.

him on particular drills and fitness regimens. During the summer, John and his family traveled to Europe, and he went on an extra two-week detour to take a Spanish immersion class in Madrid. This year, his mom is insisting that he work with both a private SAT tutor and a private college counselor who helped his brother get into college. Jane participates in extracurriculars, too—she's part of a local soccer league in Fort Worth that combines afterschool homework help with team sports. Her mom managed to pay the uniform fee, but the team had to fundraise separately to cover the cost of transportation to and from games.

Access to out-of-school opportunities paves two very different paths for children. Enrichment spending has more than doubled among wealthy

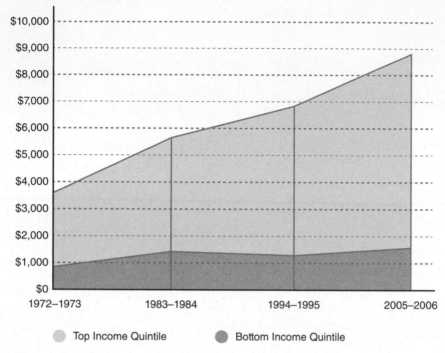

$10,000
$9,000
$8,000
$7,000
$6,000
$5,000
$4,000
$3,000
$2,000
$1,000
$0

1972–1973   1983–1984   1994–1995   2005–2006

● Top Income Quintile   ● Bottom Income Quintile

Figure 1.4 Growing Gaps in Enrichment Spending by Income Level
Source: Data from "Introduction: The American Dream, Then and Now," by Greg J.
Duncan and Richard J. Murnane, 2011, in G. J. Duncan and Richard J. Murnane
(Eds.), *Whither Opportunity? Rising Inequality, Schools, and Children's Life Chances.*
New York, NY: Russell Sage Foundation.

parents since the 1970s, whereas spending among poor parents has
increased at a far slower clip.[16] As a result, the gap between what rich
and poor parents spend has nearly tripled over the last three decades (see
Figure 1.4).

Taken together, parental time and enrichment spending are not just
testaments to income inequality: they manifest as fundamentally *social*
measures. John's parents are not just providing their child with more exotic
opportunities that money can buy. They are investing in activities that tend
to expand John's access to relationships. For many poor students like Jane,
these relationships—with college-educated family members and family
friends, tutors, coaches, and the like—remain further out of reach.

This investment gap helps explain startling disparities in access to
informal mentors, a fancy term for coaches, teachers, or parents' friends

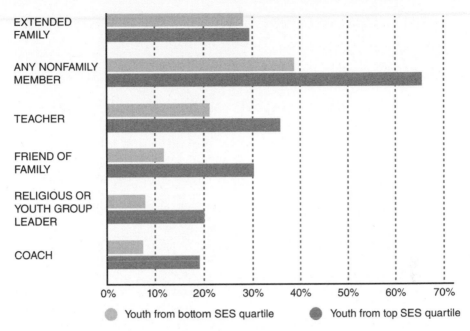

Figure 1.5 Gaps in Young People's Access to Informal Mentors by Income
Source: Data from Robert D. Putnam, *Our Kids: The American Dream in Crisis,* 2015.

gained through a student's everyday life. Low-income young people report significantly fewer informal mentors—particularly beyond their family and neighborhood—than their wealthier peers. In fact, young people from the top socioeconomic quartile report nearly *double* the rate of nonfamily adults in their lives (see Figure 1.5).

John's suite of outside-of-school activities bring the point home: his numerous basketball coaches; Spanish, math, and SAT tutors; private college counselor; and volunteer work supervisors are not just glorified babysitters—they are all part of a web of relationships surrounding John as he grows up, buoying him toward an adulthood rich with social resources. And his parents' friends in Garden City—old college friends, work colleagues, and fellow high school parents—are yet another layer of social connections at John's disposal as he looks to find his professional footing. Even with a close-knit, loving family and mentoring programs cropping up in urban centers like her hometown Fort Worth, students like Jane simply don't have access to this wide range of connections. As much love as her family and immediate community provide, Jane's web of connections is decidedly narrower, less well resourced, and less networked into the knowledge economy.

How Schools Can Address Relationship Gaps

Collectively, statistics like these paint a troubling picture. John and Jane are navigating vastly divergent constellations of social connections and inter-actions before, during, and after school.

How might society start to address these gaps? Staring down the barrel of widening income inequality in general, researchers, policymakers, and commentators from all political walks have proposed a wide range of solutions. They suggest everything from rethinking tax policy to disman-tling housing and zoning regulations, both to address the underlying causes of these gaps and to mitigate their effects on young people's prospects. We agree that structural solutions will be critical to curing underlying drivers of inequality.[17]

This book will not delve into those many ideas, compelling as they may be. We'll leave those debates to Congress, board rooms, and local town halls. Instead, we will consider a much narrower but crucial question: *How might schools address the social gaps facing American children?*

This question, of course, raises another: Why should schools care about students' networks? As the next chapter discusses in greater detail, the power of relationships is well studied in psychology, political science, and economic research alike. The research points to a single, overwhelming conclusion: social connectedness is vital to getting by and getting ahead. And research consistently underscores the particularly important role that relationships play in helping young people thrive personally, academically, and professionally.

Some of the seminal findings on this topic come from the Search Institute, a Minnesota-based social science research and public policy think tank. The late Peter Benson, former president of Search, summarized the core of the Institute's work: "After decades of forming hypotheses, conducting and publishing studies, crafting and rewriting definitions, and analyzing data, Search Institute researchers and practitioners have arrived at a surprisingly simple conclusion: nothing—*nothing*—has more impact in the life of a child than positive relationships."[18]

According to the Search Institute's comprehensive body of research, young people's connections drive their healthy development, academic success, and access to opportunity. Connections with caring adults and peers correlate with higher levels of student engagement and improved rates of academic motivation. The Search Institute's research has also shown that with greater access to developmental relationships, students tend to attain better grades, report higher aspirations, and participate more frequently in college-preparatory activities.[19] Beyond these well-studied childhood factors, being well-connected takes on a whole new meaning as young people enter adulthood. A supportive and diverse network predicts higher levels of college completion, not to mention more professional opportunity once students hit the job market.

Relationships, in other words, are at once buffers against risk and conduits to opportunity. And relationships—not just individual effort or ability—continue to play a crucial role in the sorts of activities that our meritocracy rewards. They are an inextricable variable shaping the playing field schools are asked to level.

Even more striking, however, is how much the opposite proves true. Students with weaker or smaller networks are falling behind their better-connected peers academically and professionally.

A Glimpse at the Consequences of Relationship Gaps

Students who report a lack of supportive, caring relationships are more likely to drop out and stay out of school. For example, a study by Jonathan Zaff of the nonprofit America's Promise Alliance found that young people who dropped out were far more likely to report that they had not reached out to *anyone* for help when they had trouble in school.[20] For those who reenrolled, caring adults proved to be a key driver in students' lives. In some cases, these caring adults were students' parents. But according to Zaff's surveys, teachers, mentors, coaches, siblings, or family friends could also fill the crucial role of caring for young people and motivating them to persist.

Recent research has also begun to suggest that bearing witness to harsh income inequality among adults around them is discouraging some low-income students from investing in school in the first place. In their attempt to identify what might cause students to drop out of high school, Melissa Kearney and Phillip Levine found a startling pattern: in cities or states with wide disparities between the wealth levels of the low- and middle-income brackets, high school students, particularly boys, appear more likely to drop out of school.[21]

Controlling for other factors, Kearney and Levine found that students' acute sense of hopelessness—what the researchers dubbed "economic despair"—was discouraging them from staying in school. Because those around them seemed to be lacking professional and personal opportunities, students saw little value in a high school diploma. As these authors summarized, this finding bucks how researchers typically construe opportunity and inequality: "The conventional thinking among economists is that income inequality provides incentives for individuals to invest *more* in order to achieve the higher-income position in society. But if low-income youth view middle-class life as out of reach, they might decide to invest *less* in their own economic future."[22]

Economic despair appears in geographies suffering the highest, most extreme degrees of inequality, where low-income students can't see a middle-class future based on the adults living and working (or *not* working) around them. But network gaps can also affect those low-income students who continue to invest in their education, graduate, and try to make their way to and through college. In a postrecession world, this investment in their human capital is not just prudent but necessary: nearly 75 percent of the 11.6 million jobs created during the recovery have gone to college-educated workers.[23] This new reality has grave implications for low-income students' prospects in the economy. As of 2017, according to the US Department of Education, by age twenty-five half of Americans from high-income families held a bachelor's degree compared to just one in ten from low-income families.[24]

Gaps in access to guidance counselors and in exposure to parents or informal mentors who have attended college can in part explain disparities in college matriculation between rich and poor students. But even those low-income students who defy the odds and make it to college still remain far less likely to graduate down the line. Students hailing from low-income families where neither parent earned a bachelor's degree are significantly more likely than those with a college-educated parent to leave before their second year of college.[25] And this gap is growing, not subsiding: the college completion rate among children from high-income families has grown sharply in the last few decades, far outpacing that of students from low-income families.[26]

A range of factors—including academic performance and access to financial aid—contributes to these startling attrition rates. But research suggests that lack of information and advice, lack of social supports, and a tenuous sense of belonging on college campuses appear to play a big role. Once students make it out of poor neighborhoods to college, some struggle to find their place.[27] Regardless of whether students are prepared academically—even, that is, if their talent and effort make them competitive on paper—social barriers can remain potent drivers of attrition. The inverse is also true—if a student feels a sense of social belonging and support, he's far more likely to persist. And at college, relationships with mentors are not the only powerful ties to keep students in school. Some researchers even suggest that, at this stage, peer groups (or lack thereof) wield the greatest impact on students' academic and personal development.[28]

Unsurprisingly, the benefits of stronger networks continue from there. Take hiring patterns for entry-level jobs at elite firms: specifically at law, consulting, and investment banking firms, social ties remain a key sorting mechanism among managers. In her sweeping look at how top-tier managers filter job applications, Princeton sociologist Lauren Rivera found that, by and large, to even have their resume *considered,* students needed either to attend a university with preexisting ties to a firm or have a *personal connection* to someone at the company. Both of these, of course, are strongly associated with parental socioeconomic status, and the latter with the network to which students have access. Resumes that didn't fit into one or both categories were not reviewed seriously, if at all.

As one of Rivera's interview subjects said, "There are plenty of smart people out there, we just refuse to look at them."[29] Michael Young, suffice it to say, is probably turning in his grave.

Investing in Students' Social Capital

In short, relationships function as a key driver behind schools' core priorities, such as graduation and academic outcomes. They are also a driver of education systems' bigger aspirations for their students: successful postsecondary education, access to an array of professional opportunities, and long-term health.

Taken together, emerging statistics on relationship gaps should serve as a loud wake-up call. Access to relationships will need to become a key element of school design for any school hoping to meaningfully level the playing field of opportunity.

Of course, investing in relationships cannot cure all the effects of income inequality—other policies will need to address income gaps and the hardships that poverty inflicts on childhood. But relationships do offer *real value*. As it turns out, social connections actually function as a form of capital much in the way that human and financial capital does. That value, however, is routinely underestimated in the current education system, which focuses so much on what students know (their human capital) that it risks forgetting about whom students know (their social capital).

In the next chapter, we'll unpack the concept of social capital. We will explore exactly how networks form, why they contain value, and how students—especially those on the wrong side of relationship gaps—stand to benefit from that value in the long run.

KEY TAKEAWAYS

- Belief in meritocracy is alive and well in the US. We rely heavily on our schools to play the role of "great equalizer" to ensure the health of our meritocracy. But schools are confronting a complex set of opportunity gaps emerging across students' lives.
- By many accounts, economic inequality and mobility are getting worse in America. These realities are yielding disparate childhoods, as neighborhood demographics, parental time spent with children, and enrichment spending all diverge across economic class and parental education level.

- These disparities signal that academic gaps aren't the only factor threatening equality of opportunity. Yet children's relationship and network gaps often go unaddressed. If schools hope to level the playing field, they can no longer afford to ignore these additional inequities.

Notes

1. Young, M. D. (1994). *The rise of the meritocracy.* New Brunswick, NJ: Transaction Publishers. (Original work published 1958)
2. Isaacs, J. B. (2008). International comparisons of economic mobility. Retrieved from https://www.brookings.edu/wp-content/uploads/2016/07/02_economic_mobility_sawhill_ch3.pdf
3. Sommeiller, E., Price, M., & Wazeter, E. (2016). Income inequality in the U.S. by state, metropolitan area, and county. Retrieved from http://epi.org/107100. It's worth noting that a number of economists over the years have pushed back against income as the best proxy for gauging inequality—instead, some argue that consumption is a better measure. See Attanasio, O. P., & Pistaferri, L. (2016). Consumption inequality. *Journal of Economic Perspectives, 30*(2), 1–27. Retrieved from https://web.stanford.edu/~pista/JEP.pdf
4. Chetty, R., Grusky, D., Hell, M., Hendren, N., Manduca, R., & Narang, J. (2017). The fading American dream: Trends in absolute income mobility since 1940. *Science, 356*(6336), 398–406. Retrieved from http://www.equality-of-opportunity.org/papers/abs_mobility_paper.pdf
5. Fry, R., & Taylor, P. (2012, August 1). The rise of residential segregation by income. Retrieved from http://www.pewsocialtrends.org/files/2012/08/Rise-of-Residential-Income-Segregation-2012.2.pdf; Kearney, M. S., & Levine, P. B. (2014). *Income inequality, social mobility, and the decision to drop out of high school* (NBER Working Paper No. 20195). doi:10.3386/w20195
6. Child Trends & Opportunity Nation. (n.d.). About the Opportunity Index. Retrieved from http://opportunityindex.org/about/
7. *U.S. News & World Report.* (2016). Garden City High School: 2016 rankings. Retrieved from http://www.usnews.com/education/best-high-schools/new-york/districts/garden-city-union-free-school-district/garden-city-high-school-13695; Dunbar High School: Subject proficiency testing. Retrieved from http://www.usnews.com/education/best-high-schools/texas/districts/fort-worth-isd/dunbar-high-school-19074/test-scores
8. The phrase *opportunity equation* draws from a 2014 book by Eric Schwartz. The book, which follows Schwartz's path to building the nonprofit organization Citizen Schools, begins by chronicling the hidden inequalities that often get missed when parents and advocates focus solely on achievement gaps. Schwartz, E. (2014). *The opportunity equation: How citizen teachers are combating the achievement gap in America's schools.* Boston, MA: Beacon Press.
9. Fry and Taylor, Rise of residential segregation.
10. US Government Accountability Office. (2016, April). Better use of information could help agencies identify disparities and address racial discrimination. Retrieved from http://www.gao.gov/assets/680/676745.pdf; Rothstein, R. (2016, May 23). GAO

report on segregation misses the bigger picture [Web log post]. Retrieved from http://www.epi.org/blog/gao-report-on-segregation-misses-the-bigger-picture

11. McDonough, P. M. (2005, January). Counseling and college counseling in America's high schools. Retrieved from http://citeseerx.ist.psu.edu/viewdoc/download?doi=10.1.1.543.5670&rep=rep1&type=pdf. Increasing access to school counselors has been shown to increase college-going: adding one additional high school counselor increases four-year college enrollment by 10 percent. That is, if a typical high school serving 113 seniors hired one additional counselor, 11 more seniors would enroll in a four-year school. Hurwitz, M., & Howell, J. (2013). Measuring the impact of high school counselors on college enrollment. Retrieved from https://files.eric.ed.gov/fulltext/ED562748.pdf

12. Page, L., Avery, C., & Howell, J. (2014). A review of the role of college counseling, coaching, and mentoring on students' postsecondary outcomes. Retrieved from https://research.collegeboard.org/sites/default/files/publications/2015/1/college-board-research-brief-role-college-counseling-coaching-mentoring-postsecondary-outcomes.pdf

13. US Department of Education Office for Civil Rights. (2016, October 28). 2013–2014 civil rights data collection: A first look—Key data highlights on equity and opportunity gaps in our nation's public schools. Retrieved from www2.ed.gov/about/offices/list/ocr/docs/2013-14-first-look.pdf

14. Putnam, R. (2012, June 29). Requiem for the American dream? Unequal opportunity in America. Retrieved from https://sites.hks.harvard.edu/saguaro/pdfs/aspen_July%2010.pdf; McLanahan, S. (2004). Diverging destinies: How children are faring under the second demographic transition. *Demography*, 41(4), 607–627. Retrieved from http://prelim2009.filmbulletin.org/readings/04-Population/McLanahan.pdf

15. Putnam, R. D. (2015). *Our kids: The American dream in crisis.* New York, NY: Simon & Schuster. See also Hampton, K., Sessions Goulet, L., Rainie, L., & Purcell, K. Social networking sites and our lives: Oct. 20-Nov. 28, 2010—Facebook and social support [Data file]. Retrieved from http://www.pewinternet.org/dataset/november-2010-facebook-and-social-support/; Petev, I. D. (2013). The association of social class and lifestyles: Persistence in American sociability, 1974 to 2010. *American Sociological Review*, 78(4), 633–661. doi:10.1177/0003122413491963

16. Kornrich, S. (2016, June). Inequalities in parental spending on young children: 1972 to 2010. *AERA Open*, 2(2), 2332858416644180. doi:10.1177/2332858416644180

17. For a thoughtful look at how structures and individual efforts to increase social capital can at times work at odds, see Jean Rhodes, Mentoring in the age of inequality, *Chronicle of Evidence-Based Mentoring*, January 6, 2018. Retrieved from https://chronicle.umbmentoring.org/mentoring-age-inequality/

18. Benson, P. L. (2010). *Parent, teacher, mentor, friend: How every adult can change kids' lives.* Minneapolis, MN: Search Institute Press, 13.

19. Search Institute. (n.d.). Developmental relationships: Why do they matter? Retrieved from https://www.search-institute.org/developmental-relationships/learning-developmental-relationships/

20. Center for Promise. (2015). Don't quit on me: What young people who left school say about the power of relationships. Retrieved from http://www.americaspromise.org/report/dont-quit-me

21. Kearney, M. S., & Levine, P. B. (2016). Income inequality, social mobility, and the decision to drop out of high school. Brookings Institution. Retrieved from https://

www.brookings.edu/bpea-articles/income-inequality-social-mobility-and-the-decision-to-drop-out-of-high-school/

22. Ibid.
23. Carnevale, A. P., Jayasundera, T., & Gulish, A. (2016). America's divided recovery: College haves and have-nots. Retrieved from https://files.eric.ed.gov/fulltext/ED574377.pdf
24. US Department of Education. (n.d.). College affordability and completion: Ensuring a pathway to opportunity. Retrieved from https://www.ed.gov/college. See also Bailey, M. J., & Dynarski, S. M. (2011). Inequality in postsecondary attainment. In G. Duncan & R. Murnane (Eds.), *Whither opportunity? Rising inequality, schools, and children's life chances* (pp. 1117–1132). New York, NY: Russell Sage Foundation.
25. Choy, S. P. (2002). Access & persistence: Findings from 10 years of longitudinal research on students. Retrieved from https://files.eric.ed.gov/fulltext/ED466105.pdf; Horn, L. J. (1998). Stopouts or stayouts? Undergraduates who leave college in their first year. Statistical analysis report. Retrieved from http://files.eric.ed.gov/fulltext/ED425683.pdf
26. Bailey and Dynarski, Inequality in postsecondary attainment.
27. The Ivy League's hidden poor. *MarketWatch.* Retrieved from http://www.marketwatch.com/story/the-ivy-leagues-hidden-poor-2015-04-22
28. Kuh, G. D., Kinzie, J. L., Buckley, J. A., Bridges, B. K., & Hayek, J. C. (2006, July). What matters to student success: A review of the literature. Retrieved from https://nces.ed.gov/npec/pdf/kuh_team_report.pdf
29. Rivera, L. A. (2016). *Pedigree: How elite students get elite jobs.* Princeton, NJ: Princeton University Press.

CHAPTER TWO

Getting by with a Little Help from Our Friends

What Schools Need to Know about Social Capital

Cosmic Coincidences

It's not every day that you get the chance to meet your idol. And it's not every day that that idol takes you under his wing and launches you into an incredible career pursuing your passion.

But for Bear McCreary, that's basically what happened. McCreary is arguably one of this generation's breakout composers. He's written scores for hit TV series like *Outlander* and *The Walking Dead*. But for all his raw musical talent, McCreary, by his own account, got his first big break because of an unlikely chain of connections. It began in the coastal town of Bellingham, Washington, where McCreary grew up. As he describes it,

> In the winter of 1996, I was awarded "Student of the Month" by the local Rotary Club. I got to ditch class for an afternoon to attend the ceremony where I was introduced to the members and got a free lunch. My adolescent brain was bored beyond belief. I just sat there, listening to some old dude talk about my grades and my interests. I found myself actually yearning to be back in Social Studies! During the event, they mentioned my interest in film music and that I was curious about attending the University of Southern California, famous for its Film Scoring Program.

After the luncheon, I scrambled to get out, but I was stopped by a kind-looking gentleman who introduced himself, Joe Coons. He said he was struck by my interest in film music, because he had a friend in the industry. I must confess, even at this young age, I was a little cocky, and assumed he was about to talk about someone who scores the local news or public access weather updates.

"Have you heard of Elmer Bernstein?" he asked.

Elmer Bernstein was one of the composers I most admired! My brain jolted, as if someone jammed my finger in a light socket. I stammered some inane reply.

Joe Coons was active in the Bellingham boating community. He knew Elmer because Elmer kept his boat in the marina, and each summer, he would sail up the Canadian coast to Alaska. The cosmic coincidence is staggering. Joe arranged to send a demo tape (yes, a tape . . . remember those?) to Elmer. I put a few pieces that my high school band performed on there, but the majority of the tape was filled with cues from "The Amazing Saga of George," my in-progress film score. A few months later, I heard from Joe that Elmer was willing to sit down and chat with me the next time he came to town.

That afternoon, at the Rotary Club, I learned to never take a boring luncheon for granted. To this day, Joe Coons still gets an autographed copy of my every soundtrack album.

© 2014 Bear McCreary

McCreary would go on to work as one of Bernstein's protégés for nearly a decade until the legendary composer passed away in 2004.[1]

Bear's heartwarming tale may sound like an anomaly, a random "cosmic coincidence," to use his words. But it is also a tale of relationships transforming a self-professed bored and cocky teenager's outlook. It's a story about how an institution as simple as a local luncheon can broker new connections between two people who might otherwise not meet. And how a single mentor may change the course of our lives.

It's also a subtle testament to the fact that a *chain* of relationships is a powerful asset. We all stand to benefit from our own proverbial Elmers as professional mentors. But we also benefit from proverbial Joes who can help us find our Elmers along the way.

Given the powerful role that relationships play in our opportunity equation, the urgent question facing schools is how cosmic coincidences like Bear's might become the rule—rather than the exception—in their students' lives. How might schools take the chance out of mere chance encounters?[2] And how, in particular, can schools begin to broker new connections for those students on the wrong side of relationship gaps, whose chances of finding mentors lag their already better-connected peers?

For that to happen, schools will need to better understand the basics of relationship research. Specifically, they need to understand why exactly relationships are valuable, and how trusting relationships form over time. Although these are exceedingly broad questions, in this chapter we summarize key insights from the science behind social capital. From there, we'll explore how schools can realize the value of relationships by integrating them into their day-to-day routines.

Valuing Relationships

Few people argue against the idea that networks offer us some value. It's practically a cliché to declare that "relationships matter." More complicated, however, are the questions of *how much* and *in which circumstances* they matter. These are the sorts of inquiries that social capital scholars have been exploring for decades.

In this book, we use the term *social capital* to describe the fact that people's networks contain value. To give you a sense of the state of social capital research, some particularly colorful scholars once described social capital as a "wonderfully elastic term."[3] Other researchers gathered a total of twenty-three definitions of social capital published between 1985 and 1998 alone.[4] Setting aside those academic debates for now, for the purposes of this book, we're interested first and foremost in young people's stock of social capital. We define this as *young people's access to and ability to mobilize human connections that might help them further their potential and their goals, as those goals emerge and inevitably shift over time.*

To understand what makes relationships valuable, think about the last time you relied on someone to get something done. Maybe you asked a favor of a family member. Or you emailed a former teammate for an introduction to a potential colleague. Perhaps you just leaned on a friend for moral support. Each of these moments may feel unique based on your particular dynamic with that family member or friend. But research shows that relationships can offer four *general* advantages: the flow of information, the exertion of influence, the function of social credentialing, and the reinforcement of identity or position.[5]

These are all fancy names for the sorts of returns we tend to reap from our day-to-day networks. For example, say a former coworker tells you about a job opportunity that is not yet public. That connection is granting you access to *information* otherwise unavailable. Let's say that same friend were to take the extra step of recommending you for the position. You are benefiting from his *influence* over a decision-making process. If your friend himself is in good standing with the hiring managers, you are also enjoying the benefits of the *social credentials* that your friend's recommendation bestows. He is, after all, willing to publicly vouch for your abilities or potential. Finally, that recommendation may acknowledge or *reinforce* your own identity as a worthy member of your particular professional community.

Of course, not all four of these factors will necessarily be present in every connection a young person maintains. How researchers go about measuring the "capital" in social capital is often highly contingent on the sort of relationship at hand.

Strong Ties Make Us Stronger

One of the key metrics that researchers use to gauge the potential value of a given relationship is its strength. The strength or weakness of a given relationship—or "tie," in the language of sociologists—depends on the amount of time, emotional intensity, intimacy, and reciprocity that two people share. Not surprisingly, one way researchers cast strong ties is by identifying people who repeatedly interact with and rely on one another. A close family member or spouse with whom you live or a dear friend on whom you rely is a *strong tie*. By contrast, a friend with whom you've kept in sporadic contact or a local business owner whom you see on occasion is a *weak tie*.

Not all strong ties are positive ties, of course. But research has long shown that to develop and thrive, all people, and young people in particular, need positive strong ties. The value of these close ties, in particular in-person ties, cannot be overstated—they predict all sorts of life outcomes, such as happiness, health, and even longevity.[6]

Those working in education witness firsthand the power of strong ties in their daily interactions with young people. As described in chapter 1, even a single strong, caring tie can prove especially important for at-risk youth. And more generally, students who experience strong, positive relationships—be those with family, teachers, or mentors—get better grades, have higher aspirations, and engage in college-preparatory activities more frequently.[7]

Strong ties, however, are not the only sort of relationships that bestow value in our lives. Our strong ties often help us get by. But they alone may not suffice when it comes to getting ahead.[8]

The Surprising Strength of Weak Ties

The somewhat counterintuitive truth is that although our close-knit friends and family are more likely to look out for us, they may be *less* likely to provide us with new information or opportunities. Within a tightly knit group of close friends or family members, group members actually end up knowing the same people. These redundant ties in turn offer redundant resources.[9] People in a tight-knit group know about the same information and opportunities as one another. They often exist in an echo chamber.

Instead, it turns out that more tenuous or weak ties, which are by definition more plentiful in our lives, can offer up new opportunities or information.

Researchers did not always understand the pivotal role that weak-tie acquaintances could play in people's lives. For a long time, conventional wisdom held that the stronger the relationship, the better. But in the early 1970s, sociologist Mark Granovetter of Johns Hopkins University set out to study how social interactions impacted social mobility. To do so, he surveyed a random sample of people living in a Boston suburb who had gotten their jobs through a personal contact. To his surprise, he found that over half of the employees said that they only occasionally interacted with the contact who helped them secure their new job.[10]

Granovetter realized the powerful role that merely occasional contacts were playing: job seekers' weak ties could offer new information beyond the knowledge confined to candidates' own strong-tie networks. Observing this dynamic, Granovetter coined the catchphrase "the strength of weak ties." This truth will resonate with anyone who has gone out looking for a job. Although a lucky few may benefit directly from a parent or close friend offering them a position, many will find themselves asking for introduction upon introduction until a series of ever-looser ties brings a new opportunity within reach.[11] In Bear McCreary's case, Joe was a weak tie—indeed, barely an acquaintance he ran into at a luncheon—who ended up brokering an opportunity that would last a lifetime.

The Spectrum of Our Connections

It bears noting that strong and weak ties offer a mental model for thinking about gradations of connections. But sorting our relationships into these buckets can also risk oversimplifying the more jagged realities of our social lives. Recent research continues to surface surprising nuances in the distinction between so-called strong and weak ties.

For example, our strong ties, with whom we are theoretically closest, are not necessarily those we rely on for support in every situation or circumstance. Harvard sociologist Mario Luis Small studied whom graduate students turned to when coping with life's twists and turns. Small discovered that, contrary to popular belief, these students were more likely to confide in *weak* ties than turn to their closest, strong ties. In some of these cases, subjects were going through things that nobody in their closest-knit networks had gone through, so seeking out weak ties marked an effort to find empathy for their circumstances. In others, the risks associated with divulging a struggle or misstep felt much higher with a close friend or family member than with a near stranger. Small found, in other words, that sometimes we don't actually want to confide in our allegedly closest confidants.[12]

In another body of emerging research, Tufts University professor Laura Gee has shown that although, as Granovetter discovered, most people tend to find jobs through weak ties, a single strong tie can prove more valuable all else being equal.[13] Poring over reams of deidentified Facebook data, Gee and her team determined that the stronger a given existing relationship became, the more likely subjects were to end up working with that friend. These findings, the researchers suggested, could be explained by the fact that people tend to have far more weak ties—acquaintances, former colleagues, friends of friends—than they do strong ties, but that stronger ties may be more willing to help.

These are just a few studies that reveal the complexity of calibrating the value of different ties in our lives. Our strongest positive ties tend to look out for us (and we for them) and can offer the greatest access to professional opportunities. Our weaker positive ties, however, tend to be more plentiful, and as such can diversify our access to opportunities beyond what our far fewer strong ties can offer. Our weaker ties may also provide a low-risk space to vent or grapple with our struggles.

Schools looking to shore up students' networks will need to tackle both ends of this spectrum, taking into account the many nuances in between. They will need to ensure that students have access to strong ties who help them get by emotionally, physically, financially, and academically. They will also, however, need to think creatively about expanding students' access to weak ties who might broaden the range of possibilities on students' horizons and open the door to new opportunities and connections.

To some, this might sound like a relatively feasible task. Schools could aim to connect students to more people by simply opening their doors or hosting luncheons similar to those at the Rotary Club, where Bear met Joe.

It's true that part of the solution is simply to increase students' chances of meeting new and interesting people. Valuable relationships, however, are grounded in trust, not just logistics. As American educator Stephen Covey once wrote, "Trust is the glue of life. It's the most essential ingredient in effective communication. It's the foundational principle that holds all relationships—marriages, families, and organizations of every kind—together."[14] Strengthening strong ties and diversifying weak ties will hinge on an understanding of the psychology behind how trust forms and tethers people together over time. And research shows that far and away one of the most important factors found to generate trust in social networks—particularly among our closest ties—is a little talked about but ubiquitous phenomenon known as *homophily*.

Homophily's Stronghold on Networks

Homophily describes the inclination of individuals to connect to others like themselves. In layman's terms: birds of a feather flock together. It's because of this tendency, researchers argue, that on average people's personal networks tend to be highly homogeneous along such dimensions as gender, education, religion, age, occupation, and race and ethnicity.[15] By way of example, the average white American's friend network is over 90 percent white. The average black American's friend network is over 80 percent black.[16]

Similarity breeds connection and trust, and homophily is thus something of a fact of life. It is not inherently bad or evil. Such social preferences, however, can manifest as the worst aspects of our social struggles with racism, xenophobia, and sexism. For anyone concerned with growing inequalities across the country, homophily should be approached with caution and nuance.

Our tendency to trust those similar to ourselves helps explain why young people benefit from role models who look like them or share their cultural or ethnic identity. These relationships can prove critical to shaping a positive identity and inspire a crucial sense of belonging in students' schools and communities.[17] But social capital research also reveals a second powerful truth: *the categories by which we self-sort are, at least to a degree, malleable.* For example, General Social Survey (GSS) data suggests that over the past decades, individuals have become more likely to forge close connections based on education level, and slightly less likely to form close friendships on the basis of such factors as race and religion.[18]

Changes in the influence of these factors show how homophily may drive connections along certain common dimensions. But at the same time, these ties can build bridges across other dimensions where two people may be different.[19]

Over time, survey data like the GSS holds up a powerful mirror to those categories that people consider "socially salient" when forming their closest networks.[20] The attributes that we care about—and therefore sort ourselves along—can change as personal and cultural patterns and preferences shift. To use an absurd example: were favorite ice cream flavor to suddenly become a "socially salient" category, we would see people sort themselves around ice cream preferences over other social categories such as religion and class. Suddenly we would find all of the mint chocolate chip aficionados congregating, and people would stratify across strawberry and cookie dough lines.

In other words, holding homophily constant, different dimensions of similarity can inspire trust. Maybe someone looks like you or shares your culture or religion. Maybe someone has shared experiences to which you can relate. Or maybe someone just has the same hobby as you do.

All told, the fact that similarity breeds connections is a powerful consideration when working to expand or enrich students' networks. On the one hand, homophily helps explain why young people will gravitate toward and benefit from role models with whom they can identify. On the other, understanding homophily can help schools and mentoring organizations pair students and mentors along a variety of dimensions.

When a young person meets a new person—whether it's a peer or a teacher or an old man at a Rotary Club luncheon—he will be most likely to trust that person if he can see or experience similarities to his own identity. And compelling emerging research is showing that our institutions—from schools to neighborhoods, from online to offline communities—can expand the attributes along which trusting relationships form.

Institutional Designs Can Make—or Break—Our Networks

Institutions create the opportunity for connections to form that otherwise might not occur in the course of people's lives. One of the leading scholars behind this insight is the aforementioned Harvard sociologist Mario Luis Small. In a sweeping study documented in his 2009 book *Unanticipated Gains,* Small found that some child-care centers in New York City created enduring opportunities for parents—particularly mothers—to repeatedly engage in child-centered activities, including field trips and party planning. Through such repeated activities, the mothers themselves began to form ties. Crucially, this suggested that the shared experience of motherhood, paired with the particular institutional designs of care centers, could inspire relationships that crossed neighborhood, race, and class lines.

These relationships did not always go deeply into their personal lives. But mothers trusted other mothers with whom they repeatedly interacted, even in small spurts.[21]

In other words, institutions can make it more likely that two people will connect, regardless of their apparent differences. This can impact even our tendency to self-sort along certain demographic dimensions. For example, in a study of student and recent graduate networks at Dartmouth College, economists found that two randomly chosen white students interacted three times more often than did a randomly chosen black student and a randomly chosen white student. However, the college's deliberate designs among first-year students could shift these patterns: if a black and a white student lived in the same freshman dorm, the frequency with which they interacted increased by a factor of three.[22]

Institutions can also increase the likelihood of what we might otherwise deem to be "chance encounters." Although many would describe Bear's encounter with Joe as some mix of his dumb luck and raw talent, a social capital scholar might see something else afoot: the Rotary Club where Bear met Joe played a crucial intervening role in forging a new connection that would send Bear on a promising path in his music career. By creating a space where older community members could learn about local students' interests and abilities, the luncheon offered a structure in which new ties—even beyond those in the room—could take root.

Put simply, institutions from child-care centers to college dorms to Rotary Clubs can drive the formation of social capital that would be unlikely to develop in their absence.

Schools are no different. As core institutions in their communities, with the *right designs* schools have the potential to dramatically shape the networks at their students' disposal. By understanding the power of both strong and weak ties, and how the tendencies of homophily inspire trust, schools could play a leading role in starting to tackle long-standing relationship gaps among America's children.

To do so, schools will need to innovate. Specifically, they will need to rethink how their designs could more deliberately expand beyond just academics to integrate the positive effects of both strong and weak ties into students' lives.

Integrating Social Capital into the Architecture of School

Readers who work inside education may be wary about undertaking efforts to invest in students' social capital. This could end up as yet another in an endless list of tasks piled onto teachers' and administrators' plates. Luckily, innovation theory suggests that these efforts could offer a huge payoff. By investing in the social resources at students' disposal, schools could start to produce breakthrough academic and postsecondary outcomes for their students.[23] The very results, in fact, that previous decades of reform have struggled to produce.

Put simply, by integrating more factors that influence students' lives into their designs, schools stand to boost performance. This phenomenon is actually well studied beyond education. Across industries, when firms are trying to improve dramatically, they often wrap their arms around the various and sundry components that stand to impact performance.

All products, services, and systems have an architecture, or design, that determines what its parts are and how they must interact with each other. The place where any two parts fit together is called an interface. In circumstances where organizations are aiming to radically improve the performance of their products and services, integrating across these interfaces is crucial. When organizations do this, they are pursuing a particular structure: an *interdependent architecture.*

A service's architecture is *interdependent* if the way one part is designed, made, and delivered depends on the way other parts are designed, made, and delivered—and vice versa. Successful enterprises pursue interdependent architectures when they want to improve a product, service, or entire industry.

Take Gustavus Franklin Swift's innovative approach to marketing beef in the late nineteenth century.

In Swift's day, beef was sold on a strictly local basis. At the time, butchers couldn't ensure that the meat could stay fresh over long train rides to far-flung customers. But Swift was determined to create an economy of scale: he centralized butchering in Kansas City, which meant he could process beef at a very low cost. Then Swift designed the world's first ice-cooled railcars so that his wares could remain fresh over long distances. In other words, because there was no way to outsource distribution, Swift had to become a refrigeration maverick—not just a beef butcher—in order to innovate. By building a business in which butchering and transporting beef were interdependent, he was able to revolutionize the beef industry as a whole.

The phenomenon of interdependent architectures driving breakthrough performance holds true in other industries as well. For example, in the early days of the computing industry, tweaks to any one part of a computer—such as the operating system, core memory, or logic circuitry—would impact all the others. To build the best machines in the world, industry leaders like IBM could not merely assemble mainframe computers from prefabricated parts. Instead, IBM had to control the *entirety* of production to build better and better-performing machines.[24] In other words, it had to produce operating systems, core memory, and the like in house (see Figure 2.1).

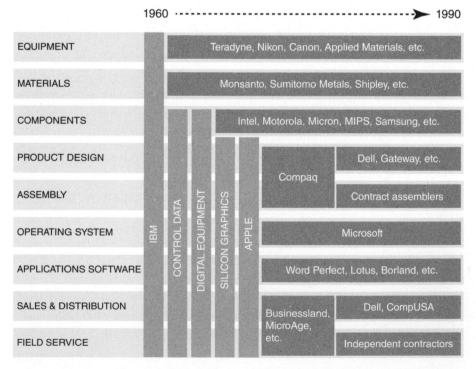

Figure 2.1 Integration and Modularity in the Computer Industry over Thirty Years

Companies and industries rarely remain in a highly integrated state forever. Over time they modularize. This occurs once a product meets or exceeds customers' demands. Then, and only then, could IBM begin to define and outsource discrete component parts. Unlike in an interdependent architecture, in a *modular* architecture, there are no unpredictable interdependencies in the design of the service's parts. Modular parts fit and work together in well-understood, crisply codified ways. Modular components can be developed in independent work groups or by different organizations working at arm's length.[25] Modular architectures, while limiting firms' ability to innovate to new heights, optimize for efficiency and flexibility. Customers can mix and match modular parts to customize to their liking.

Why Schools' Modular Architecture Costs Students

Schools may feel far afield from personal computer manufacturers or beef distribution channels, but there is at least one important similarity. Many schools, particularly those serving low-income and minority students, are not producing the great results that policies or the public hopes and expects of them. Schools falling short on performance find themselves in a similar "not good enough" position as IBM did in the early days of the mainframe computer and Swift did as he struggled to expand his business beyond Kansas City stockyards.

Through the lens of theory, our decades-long struggle to close race- and income-based achievement gaps suggests that schools may be living the consequences of a system that has prematurely modularized. The different components that make up a student's life chances and academic success—health care, support services, academics, diverse networks, and the like—currently fit into stubborn silos. Strict interfaces separate what happens inside school from what happens beyond it. All the while, out-of-school and nonacademic factors inevitably contribute to student performance.

This "modular" architecture severely hamstrings schools' ability to innovate toward better outcomes for all students.

Outcomes, of course, is a loaded term in schools today. However wide-ranging our ambitions as a society are, in recent decades standardized test scores have become the de facto metric for judging how well the nation's schools are performing. And against these albeit narrow measures, although low-income students and their higher-income peers have both posted gains, the achievement gap between these groups has barely budged over the past decades.[26] In recent decades, data on similarly troubling gaps has emerged further down the line when it comes to access to opportunity among poor adolescents and young adults: only 9 percent of low-income students earn a bachelor's degree by their mid-twenties, compared to 77 percent of their wealthy peers.[27]

To tackle these achievement and opportunity gaps, schools serving low-income populations would benefit from an interdependent architecture. Schools need to integrate far beyond their core competency—delivering academics—to produce dramatically better and different results.

By this logic, in light of the gaps described in chapter 1, schools will need to tackle the social aspects of students' lives. They will need to adopt a new, interdependent architecture that integrates the value of strong- and weak-tie relationships into their designs.

This is obviously easier said than done. Investing in students' strong ties that can offer sources of care or support can prove daunting. School systems often lack the capacity and funding to offer a wide array of nonacademic services. And establishing coherent and effective partnerships across youth services providers and with students' families and communities poses a formidable challenge. Public policies often create silos that separate academic services from other supports, such as community-based mentorship, health care, or family support services. Disparate funding streams in turn constrain schools' abilities to incorporate these services into their existing systems and processes in an interdependent way.

Integrating access to a diverse array of weak-tie relationships into the architecture of school may also introduce potentially difficult logistical challenges. Not to mention that the more connections a school facilitates, the greater the possible risk to children's safety and privacy.

But the potential on the other side of an interdependent architecture is immense. Just as theory would predict, schools that are beginning to integrate social supports and deepen students' networks are producing breakthrough results that have long eluded schools, especially those serving low-income and minority students. In the following chapters, we outline emerging innovations that stand to strengthen students' strong-tie networks and diversify their weak-tie networks.

KEY TAKEAWAYS

- Researchers define the concept of social capital in various ways. We refer to social capital as the value of the resources and benefits contained in an individual's network. Specifically in the course of this book, we define this as young people's access to and ability to mobilize human connections to help them reach their potential.
- People need both strong and weak ties in their lives. Education reformers seeking to boost outcomes for low-income students tend to focus on strong ties—caring adults such as parents, teachers, and mentors. Although these ties are crucial, schools should also recognize the "strength of weak ties." Weak ties can serve as critical new conduits of information and opportunity that can help students get ahead.
- Trust is a key ingredient to relationships. Similarity breeds trust. Homophily, the tendency for similar people to be connected at a higher rate than dissimilar people, results in networks that are frequently segregated along such dimensions as race, religion, and class. The dimensions along which we self-sort, however, are malleable. Innovations that intend to diversify or strengthen networks must be built with homophily in mind.
- The architecture of a company or an entire industry will often cycle between relatively interdependent and modular architectures depending on what customers demand: more performance or greater customizability. When performance is falling short, companies tend to pursue interdependent architectures in order to innovate to new heights. When performance is "good enough," firms and industries tend to standardize and modularize.

- An interdependent architecture that controls more variables shaping performance can lead to breakthrough results. Schools need to "integrate backward" to address students' access to both strong and weak ties. Theory suggests that this move could dramatically increase schools' performance against measures of academic achievement and access to opportunity.

Notes

1. McCreary, B. (2014). My decade with Elmer Bernstein. Copyright 2014 by Bear McCreary. Reprinted with permission. Retrieved from http://www.bearmccreary .com/#blog/blog/other/my-decade-with-elmer-bernstein-3/
2. We credit social entrepreneur (and good friend) Eric Wilson with this powerful phrase of taking the chance out of chance encounters. Wilson is the CEO of Noble Impact, an Arkansas-based nonprofit aimed at expanding students' access to opportunity.
3. Lappé, F. M., & Du Bois, P. M. (1997). Building social capital without looking backward. *National Civic Review, 86*(2), 119–128. doi:10.1002/ncr.4100860205
4. Adler, P. S., & Kwon, S. W. (2002). Social capital: Prospects for a new concept. *Academy of Management Review, 27*(1), 17–40. doi:10.5465/AMR.2002.5922314
5. Lin, N. (2002). *Social capital: A theory of social structure and action.* Cambridge, UK: Cambridge University Press.
6. Pinker, S. (2014). *The village effect: How face-to-face contact can make us healthier and happier.* Toronto, Canada: Random House Canada. Robert Putnam's research has likewise identified the impact that strong social capital has on health, particularly when it comes to group membership. Any aging smokers should take note: "As a rough rule of thumb, if you belong to no groups but decide to join one, you cut your risk of dying over the next year in half," he wrote. "If you smoke and belong to no groups, it's a toss-up statistically whether you should stop smoking or start joining." Putnam, R. D. (2001). *Bowling alone: The collapse and revival of American community.* New York, NY: Simon & Schuster.
7. Search Institute. (n.d.). Developmental relationships: Why do they matter? Retrieved from https://www.search-institute.org/developmental-relationships/learning-developmental-relationships/. See also Mahoney, J. L., & Vest, A. E. (2012). The over-scheduling hypothesis revisited: Intensity of organized activity participation during adolescence and young adult outcomes. *Journal of Research on Adolescence, 22*(3), 409–418. doi:10.1111/j.1532-7795.2012. 00808.x; and Olsson, C. A., McGee, R., Nada-Raja, S., & Williams, S. M. (2013). A 32-year longitudinal study of child and adolescent pathways to well-being in adulthood. *Journal of Happiness Studies, 14,* 1069–1083. doi:10.1007/s10902-012-9369-8
8. As MIT professor Xavier de Souza Briggs has noted, policymakers should pay attention to distinct forms of social capital: ties that can help us "get by" and those that help us "get ahead." de Souza Briggs, X. (1998). Brown kids in white suburbs: Housing mobility and the many faces of social capital. *Housing Policy Debate, 9*(1), 177–221. doi:10.1080/10511482.1998.9521290

9. Burt, R. S. (2000). The network structure of social capital. *Research in Organizational Behavior, 22,* 345–423. doi:10.1016/S0191-3085(00)22009-1

10. Granovetter, M. (1973). The strength of weak ties. *American Journey of Sociology, 78*(6). doi:10.1086/225469

11. Despite these findings, Granovetter and others, such as Sandra Susan Smith of UC Berkeley, have shown that poor adults do not leverage weak ties to access opportunities for upward job mobility as they do for lateral job mobility. See Smith, S. S. (2016). Job-finding among the poor: Do social ties matter? In D. Brady & L. M. Burton (eds.), *The Oxford handbook of the social science of poverty.* Oxford, UK: Oxford University Press. However, schools should note that Granovetter and others have pointed out that there is a significant education–weak-tie interaction; the benefits of weak ties appear to increase with higher levels of education.

12. Small, M. L. (2017). *Someone to talk to.* New York, NY: Oxford University Press.

13. Gee, L. K., Jones, J., & Burke, M. (2017). Social networks and labor markets: How strong ties relate to job finding on Facebook's social network. *Journal of Labor Economics, 35,* 485–518. doi:10.1086/686225

14. Covey, S. R., Merrill, A. R., & Merrill, R. R. (1995). *First things first.* New York, NY: Simon & Schuster.

15. McPherson, M., Smith-Lovin, L., & Cook, J. M. (2001). Birds of a feather: Homophily in social networks. *Annual Review of Sociology, 27*(1), 415–444. doi:10.1146/annurev.soc.27.1.415

16. Ingraham, C. (2014, August 25). Three quarters of whites don't have any non-white friends. *Washington Post.* Retrieved from https://www.washingtonpost.com/news/wonk/wp/2014/08/25/three-quarters-of-whites-dont-have-any-non-white-friends

17. For a good summary of the compelling research behind the relationship between students' sense of belonging and academic outcomes, see Romero, C. (2015, July). *What we know about belonging from scientific research.* Retrieved from http://mindsetscholarsnetwork.org/wp-content/uploads/2015/09/What-We-Know-About-Belonging.pdf

18. Smith, J. A., McPherson, M., & Smith-Lovin, L. (2014). Social distance in the United States: Sex, race, religion, age, and education homophily among confidants, 1985 to 2004. *American Sociological Review, 79*(3), 432–456. doi:10.1177/0003122414531776

19. As Xavier de Souza Briggs has written, "But networks, schools, workplaces, and formal associations (civic clubs, faith institutions, etc.) that 'bond' along one dimension of social identity (socioeconomic status, for example) can 'bridge' on others (race and gender, say). Such *cross-cutting ties* derive their special significance from the fact that they bond on the social trait shared by the linked actors while bridging their social differences. Cross-cutting ties are essential to the development of broader identities and communities of interest (Blau and Schwartz 1984; Briggs 2004; Horton 1995; Varshney 2002)." de Souza Briggs, X. (2007). "Some of my best friends are . . . ": Interracial friendships, class, and segregation in America. *City & Community, 6,* 263–290. doi:10.1111/j.1540-6040.2007.00228.x

20. Smith et al., Social distance in the United States.

21. Carrying this example further, Small also found that institutions like child-care centers stand to nurture "compartmental" strong ties—that is, ties that are domain specific and that may not permeate each intimate corner of our lives as would a family member or a close friend, but that nonetheless become and remain strong. Small, M. L. (2009). *Unanticipated gains: Origins of network inequality in everyday life.* New York, NY: Oxford University Press.

22. These findings suggest that physical proximity and shared experiences are salient sorting factors for friendships between students. Marmaros, D., & Sacerdote, B. (2006). How do friendships form? *Quarterly Journal of Economics, 121*(1), 79–119. doi:10.1093/qje/121.1.79

23. This section draws on a 2015 white paper published by the Clayton Christensen Institute. Horn, M., & Freeland, J. (2015). *The educator's dilemma.* Retrieved from https://www.christenseninstitute.org/publications/the-educators-dilemma

24. It bears noting that the theory of integration and modularity turns on the concept of causation. Put in different terms, when parts of a value chain are unpredictably interdependent, causal connections between various parts are not well understood. In an education system, for example, if practitioners deploy a range of inputs to support student outputs, but they do not know which of those inputs drove student outcomes, the moving parts of this system remain unpredictably interdependent.

25. Unlike interdependent architectures, modular architectures optimize flexibility, which allows for easy customization. Because people can exchange pieces without redesigning everything else, customizing for different needs or tastes is relatively easy. A modular architecture enables an organization to serve these needs. Modularity also opens the system to enable competition for performance improvement and cost reduction of each module. That said, because modular architectures require tight specification, they allow for fewer degrees of freedom in the design of the system itself. As a result, modularity comes at the sacrifice of raw performance.

26. The Nation's Report Card. (2013). Have achievement gaps changed? Trend in fourth-grade NAEP mathematics average scores and score gaps, by race/ethnicity. Retrieved from http://www.nationsreportcard.gov/reading_math_2013/#/achievement-gaps

27. Cahalan, M., & Perna, L. (2015). *Indicators of higher education equity in the United States: 45 year trend report.* Pell Institute for the Study of Opportunity in Higher Education. Retrieved from https://eric.ed.gov/?id=ED555865. These gaps crop up even after low-income students have made it across the finish line of high school and been admitted into college. An estimated 22 percent of low-income students who were "college-intending" at high school graduation "melted" during the summer (never showed up to college). See Castleman, B. L., & Page, L. C. (2014). A trickle or a torrent? Understanding the extent of summer "melt" among college-intending high school graduates. *Social Science Quarterly, 95*(1), 202–220. doi:10.1111/ssqu.12032

CHAPTER THREE

There's No App for That

The Power of Integrating Access to Strong Ties and Care

Love Leads the Way

The Center for Advanced Learning, known simply as CAL, is not exactly situated at a hub of opportunity. The school is located in an area of Los Angeles where the territories of no fewer than fourteen rival street gangs intersect. It has been forced to lock down because of gunfire in the neighborhood, sometimes right across the street. Ninety percent of CAL's K–5 students qualify for free and reduced lunch, and many come from single-parent households. Yet, against an undeniably challenging backdrop, lifted up by the care and unconditional support of CAL's teachers and administrators, the children are safe, and many are thriving academically.[1]

"Our families work incredibly hard, but they are not always able to give their kids what they would really want them to have or even have it for themselves," CAL third-grade teacher Johanna Parker said during a November 2016 appearance on the hit daytime television show *Ellen*, hosted by Ellen DeGeneres. "Here at CAL we're teaching our students to make good choices. They know that we believe in them. That they can become the doctors, the lawyers, whatever they want to be, they can become, and those are the things that we instill in our students," principal Brooke Jackson explained. "From the time that they walk into our doors, they are greeted, and loved, and respected, and cherished and encouraged to be the best versions of themselves possible," said Parker.

DeGeneres surprised the guests (which as any Ellen fan knows, she tends to do often) by revealing that forty CAL students were actually there on the set of the show. The teacher and principal screamed with delight as the children swarmed around them. Watching them embrace, you get the sense that Jackson and Parker treat their students as they would their own children. Principal Jackson summed it up: "Our school, when you walk through the doors, exudes love," she said.

Transcending Challenges with Care

Examples like CAL illustrate the simple fact that children, particularly younger children, *need* in-person care and support. In the most basic sense, caring adults provide physical safety and security for young children. But they also, as Jackson and Parker attest, provide young people access to reliable, stable sources of care—and love—in order for those children to thrive.

Resource and care gaps facing different student populations have always posed a thorny challenge to school systems. Schools, however, should not shy away from the power that providing more care, love, and support can offer. Indeed, innovation theory describing the power of interdependent architectures suggests that if schools hope to produce breakthrough results, they will need to integrate social supports alongside academic ones.

Integrating backward into nonacademic areas of students' lives can effectively allow schools to address chronic barriers to learning. Specifically, tackling performance head on requires understanding the resources and care flowing through students' most intimate, strong-tie networks: their families and caregivers. In circumstances where students' families are unable to provide sufficient care, resources, or both, schools will need to expand their designs to support students and families in a more comprehensive manner. Not doing so will gravely limit schools' ability to close academic achievement and opportunity gaps.

Depending on their family circumstances, some children may experience a gap in caring relationships. Others may have plenty of caring relationships in their lives but lack the resources necessary to support healthy care and development. Without ensuring that students have access to *both* these foundational caring relationships and crucial resources, the best academic approaches in the world may fall short.

With this in mind, a number of school systems are successfully adopting an interdependent approach. These integrated approaches supply students with numerous nonacademic supports within a new architecture of schooling. In the field, such approaches are often referred to broadly as "wraparound services" models or "community schools" models. More recently, researchers have described them as "integrated student supports." Although a range of such approaches exists, one model stands out among the rest: an organization called City Connects, based in Boston, Massachusetts. City Connects demonstrates the immense potential of schools integrating backward to provide a web of care and supports—beyond merely academic supports—to ensure that more students can learn and thrive.

City Connects: Constructing an Individualized Network of Care

The goal of City Connects is to mitigate the effects of poverty on students' academic achievement and life chances.[2] The organization officially began in 2001 through a partnership among researchers at Boston College, teachers and administrators at a Boston public elementary school, and leaders at local Boston-based community service organizations.[3] Its guiding philosophy, however, took root long before that. Decades earlier, City Connects founder and Boston College psychology professor Mary Walsh began spending time in hospitals and community schools interviewing children and sharing what she learned with their doctors and teachers.

In these settings, Walsh observed a profound disconnect between the challenges facing children and the systems designed to address those challenges. To address this disconnect, she witnessed firsthand the power of strengthening relationships between students and teachers, by arming teachers with knowledge about what was happening in their students' lives beyond the classroom. "As we described what we had learned about the children, the teachers would have these ah-ha moments. The information really changed how the teachers thought about their students right in front of my eyes," Walsh recalled. At the same time, Walsh began to see that teachers and principals routinely struggled to coordinate care and support to meet the needs of individual students. "The grossly neglected part of schools has always been student supports," she said. "There has been no systemic practice that counselors and social workers followed."

City Connects grew out of these initial insights in an effort to surface and tackle barriers to learning facing poor children. The program began over an intensive two-year planning process in six schools in a neighborhood spanning Boston's Allston, Brighton, and Mission Hill areas. Today, City Connects operates in one hundred schools in five states, and has begun adapting its model for both early childhood centers and community colleges.

To address barriers to learning in children's lives, the program coordinates relationships among community partners, social services agencies, schools, and teachers. (See Figure 3.1.) The model hinges on knowing individual kids and families well enough to provide them with the exact sorts of care and supports that they need to thrive. To do so, City Connects

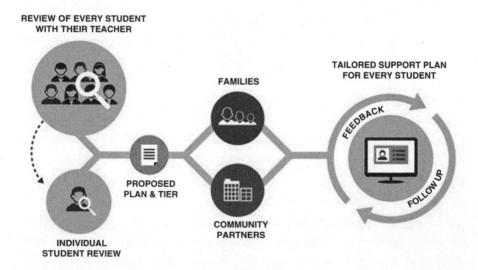

Figure 3.1 Visualizing the City Connects Model

Source: From "Our Approach," by City Connects, n.d. Retrieved from http://www.bc.edu/bc-web/schools/lsoe/sites/cityconnects/our-approach.html

plants school site coordinators (SSCs) inside schools. SSCs are typically master's-level school counselors or social workers. They are not seen as separate from the rest of the school staff. Rather, they become an integral part of the school and forge strong relationships with teachers, leaders, students, and parents to effectively broker supports for individual students depending on their particular circumstances.

At the beginning of the school year, teachers meet with these coordinators to discuss the individual developmental strengths and weaknesses of *each and every* student in the class. These conversations span across several domains: students' academic, social-emotional, health, and family circumstances. Then, within each domain, SSCs tier the child's level of risk ranging from "minimal risk" to "severe risk." Using this profile, and working in conjunction with family members and school administrators, teachers and coordinators then create an individualized support plan for each student. The plan leverages a network of relationships and supports drawing on a combination of community- and school-based resources. SSCs also connect students to a tailored set of enrichment programs, such as athletics and after-school programs. Students with more complex needs receive an Individual Student Review, which brings a team of appropriate professionals around the table to develop a support plan.

From there, the program and corresponding interventions evolve alongside students. To continuously respond to changes in students' lives, City Connects touches base with teachers on a regular basis throughout the school year and revisits and modifies the support plans when the child is not making adequate progress. To track student progress, coordinators use a proprietary database developed by City Connects—the Student Support Information System (SSIS).[4]

The City Connects model may sound akin to many an intervention and risk-assessment program in schools today. Walsh, however, is careful to distinguish the City Connects model from typical approaches that schools tend to pursue. "Someone said to me once, 'You're connectors.' But that's too mechanical," she said. "This thing isn't mechanical. It's knowing the child, and knowing the parent. That way, his teacher may say, 'Gee, I think he'd be great down the street at this program.' But the coordinator may say, 'His mom works in the other direction. If we send him there, it's going to make it tough for her.'" The "Connect" in City Connects, in other words, does not merely connote understanding particular categories of student challenges and matching them with solutions, as would an algorithm. Rather, the model aims to understand the whole of a student's life. From there, his school can attend to his needs in a manner that is sensitive to his particular circumstances. It hinges, in other words, on the adults helping to facilitate supports actually *knowing* the student and his family.

In keeping with this degree of individualization, City Connects does not sort students in the manner that many school-based interventions tend to, by grouping students into cohorts based on their risk profiles. "We work with every single teacher. And we work with every single child, with a tailored plan," Walsh said.

And that, Walsh hypothesizes, is part of what makes City Connects one of the most effective research-based models of integrated student supports in the country. In a study of nearly eight thousand K–5 students over a ten-year period from 1999 to 2009, researchers found that children enrolled in schools affiliated with City Connects outperformed comparison peers in elementary school report card scores.[5] These gains are greatest for children who spend the most time in City Connects schools, demonstrating a credible "dosage effect."[6]

Promising results then follow students over time. After leaving, students who attended City Connects elementary schools outperformed peers on middle school state tests and the Stanford Achievement Test.[7] City Connects effects are especially pronounced for English Language Learners, who by third grade score similarly on reading report card scores to students in comparison schools proficient in English.[8] Relatedly, immigrant students exposed to City Connects outperform immigrant peers never enrolled in a City Connects school on standardized math and English tests.[9] These outcomes hold across multiple sites. And the researchers guiding these efforts are also consistently finding positive effects on student outcomes using a wide variety of increasingly sophisticated analytical methods.[10] The effects of the intervention remain robust over time: students who attended a City Connects school from grades K–5 were about half as likely to drop out of high school as comparison peers.

Relationships at the Core

What seems to be driving City Connects' impressive results? Walsh is the first to admit that untangling what precisely is driving these outcomes—among the array of interventions that the model puts in place—is a tricky task. She hypothesizes, however, that just as her early work in community schools and hospitals suggested, relationships are playing a role. City Connects may be driving positive academic outcomes not just because it provides crucial poverty relief services to high-need students, as do a number of other intervention models, but also because, by design, it helps the schools and teachers matching students with those supports to fundamentally know their students and their families better.

"The heart of the relationship in what we do is the teacher-student relationship," she said. "Many teachers will say of course I love all my kids, but there are some kids for whom they don't know exactly how to explain their challenging behavior or lack of academic progress. Teachers tell us 'City Connects changed my understanding of where this child is coming from. It helped to explain his performance or behavior. I thought it was X, and now I realize that it was Y + Z.'"

It also bears noting that *care* is a loaded term. Schools attempting to connect students to care will need to beware of the ugliest versions of doing so, in which institutions adjudicate care with limited evidence or step in to "assimilate" children to new or different cultures that break with that of their family. For this reason, the most powerful of these models include and integrate with the family—rather than rejecting or excluding parents and guardians from the project of care.[11] City Connects manages to do this by triangulating among the teacher, student, and family when hatching each individual student plan.

From there, an additional web of relationships can also spring forth. Because they're not tied to one grade level, SSCs themselves often get to know children over the course of multiple years. They also broker continuous interaction among community agencies. "Johnny doesn't walk in cold to a Boys and Girls Club," Walsh said. "The coordinator has already provided the agency with the context on his needs. Instead, he goes in there a known quantity." This again suggests the nuance of integrating across different student programs at the level of the individual student, rather than merely connecting a student and a program across a predetermined interface, like a plug into an outlet.

Covering the Costs of Care

At this point, we expect many readers are nodding along—of course care and supports drive better outcomes. Of course more social workers and risk assessments could improve academic achievement. Those and other readers, however, are likely wondering about one tiny but very important detail: cost. A human "integrator" who can understand the particular needs of a child and introduce him more seamlessly into new environments would sound like a luxury to most schools. Schools might want to tailor services more diligently and personally to each student, but looking at their budgets, have little capacity to do so.

Put differently, in a resource-constrained policy environment in which education must consistently compete for funding with everything from local infrastructure projects to un- or partially funded pension obligations, is a wraparound service model cost-effective? Won't integrating additional supports simply break the bank?

Those districts that work with City Connects have managed to pay for the model either out of central funds or with a mix of central funds and corporate and foundation grants. Are these investments proving worthwhile?

One way of tackling this question is to weigh an intervention's benefits against its costs. All things considered, bean-counting school boards or legislators might argue that interventions like these are worth implementing only if they are adequately efficient, as measured by their benefit-cost ratio—hopefully greater than 1, but ideally much larger. Fortunately for this analysis, a 2015 study produced by researchers from Columbia University's Center for Benefit-Cost Studies of Education (CBCSE) applied just this sort of "efficiency test" to City Connects' specific approach.[12]

Complexity abounds in these sorts of analyses, so it's worth running through some of the details. To calculate costs, the researchers estimated and tallied up the value of all costs associated with the intervention's various "ingredients." These included such costs as volunteer time, space, and personnel salaries. To ensure that all costs were captured, they estimated and tallied these expenses regardless of whether they were incurred by schools, community agencies, or City Connects itself. To calculate benefits, they modeled the impact of the intervention's effect on standardized test scores and high school dropout rates. They also incorporated other factors, such as future incarceration rates, the anticipated level of dependence on public assistance for students receiving City Connects services, and the estimated effect of the intervention on students' lifetime earnings.[13]

The results are convincing. By the study's relatively conservative estimate, the benefit-to-cost ratio for City Connects, taking into account the total cost of services, was 3:1.[14] Assessing only the costs to schools, the ratio was 11:1.

The takeaway? It can be tempting to substitute lower-cost alternatives in place of more comprehensive, seemingly higher-cost interventions. We could, for example, easily imagine a more rudimentary intervention in which a district outfits each of its public schools with a few bookshelves stocked with brochures that describe the resources offered by various community agencies in the surrounding neighborhood. We could likewise imagine schools hiring "coordinators" or social workers in hopes that they might address students' needs, but not investing in partnerships with community-based service providers who might furnish students with additional supports.

Although implementing any of these apparently less expensive models might *seem* cheap and easy, such "modular" approaches ironically create poor and *costly* substitutes for the kind of truly individualized, integrated supports that students and families require.[15]

Arguably, the costs of *not* integrating backward to tackle resource and support gaps in school are in fact enormously high to society. These costs, however, typically remain hidden from the financial statements of any one organization. A modular system requires that students and families seek out support through a series of disconnected channels that are not tailored to their circumstances. In other words, rather than functioning as an information desk with prefabricated pamphlets pointing families to resources, an integrated approach like City Connects can function more akin to a "help desk" that troubleshoots for the individual student. And doing so requires that schools both know their students well and are able to direct crucial resources to those students.

Integrating Forward to Address Opportunity Gaps

How far reaching might supports need to extend in students' lives to address social gaps?

If schools successfully integrate backward to shore up the care and resources in students' strong-tie networks, they stand to make a meaningful dent in persistent achievement gaps. They likewise, however, may need to integrate forward to address barriers to opportunity that may appear down the line. Put differently, successfully lifting barriers to learning will not necessarily lift barriers to opportunity.

The sometimes-controversial example of KIPP Public Charter Schools sheds some light on this discrepancy. On the spectrum of systems adopting an interdependent school architecture, KIPP represents a fairly aggressive example. As a national network of public charter schools, KIPP schools serve primarily low-income and minority students. Its K–12 model shares many of the characteristics of City Connects. Like City Connects, KIPP schools provide numerous nonacademic supports that appear to help explain its phenomenal success in addressing achievement gaps.[16]

Test scores, however, are not the ultimate metric that the KIPP organization holds itself to. Instead, its mission is "to prepare KIPP students to succeed in college and lead choice-filled lives."[17]

Against these ambitious success metrics, as KIPP students began to enter young adulthood, a troubling pattern emerged. Leaders were dismayed to discover that despite posting impressive test score outcomes among their graduates, their students did not always fare so well after they entered college. College success, it turned out, was not a given. This was true despite the fact that KIPP was successfully getting low-income first-generation students *into* college at nearly unprecedented rates.[18]

To tackle these gaps, in recent years KIPP has integrated across the interface between high school *and* college. In a concerted effort to stem college attrition among its graduates, KIPP established the KIPP Through College program. Counselors and alumni coaches help KIPP graduates navigate the challenges of postsecondary education and even chart a career path. At colleges that serve high numbers of KIPP students, KIPP Through College establishes peer networks to ease students' social transition from high school to college.[19]

Like the supports provided by City Connects, the KIPP Through College model hinges in large part on relationships. KIPP staff keep in touch with students after they graduate from eighth grade, no matter where they end up attending high school—within the KIPP network or outside of it. For instance, as Caroline Bermudez described in a 2017 *Education Post* article, when KIPP graduate Nathan Woods, now a teacher at KIPP DC College Preparatory, couldn't afford to pay for transportation from his home back to college, KIPP teachers stepped in to drive him. Although we might be tempted to view Woods's transportation challenges purely as a resource issue, it turns out that the continued social support that KIPP students receive through college proves equally important. As Woods said, "I didn't realize how much that kept me going. It's bigger than teaching. I think that's love."[20]

Tools Expanding Access to Opportunity

KIPP's example illustrates an unsettling truth: although they are related, K–12 achievement and long-term access to opportunity are not always synonymous. Successful interventions that expand strong-tie supports and resources can lift barriers to learning and can help close achievement gaps. But better achievement test scores may still mask fragilities in students' networks, significantly curtailing these students' ability to "get ahead" in the long run. As Richard Barth, president of the KIPP Foundation, said, "Even our kids who go to the most selective colleges . . . still don't come from a world where they have the networks."[21]

This should hardly come as a surprise in light of the research on social capital summarized in chapters 1 and 2. Shoring up the strongest, most caring ties in students' lives can go a long way toward helping them develop and thrive. But evening the playing field will also hinge on investing in students' weak-tie networks that can open doors to opportunity down the line.

Arming students with broader networks that can carry them into successful college and career paths introduces a whole other set of logistical and cost questions for schools. The good news, however, is that a different sort of innovation is hovering on the horizon. Disruptive innovations that make new connections more accessible and affordable are beginning to penetrate schools. And these innovations hold the distinct promise of arming students with diverse weak-tie networks that could help students get ahead. In chapter 4, we delve into the potential of these disruptive technologies.

KEY TAKEAWAYS

- Young people can't "get ahead" if they cannot "get by." In many cases, they need strong, reliable, face-to-face ties with caring adults to do so.
- Schools aiming to boost outcomes among low-income students must be willing to address the social aspects of their students' lives—beyond just provisioning academics—if they hope to overcome barriers to learning.
- These efforts in schools often take the form of "wraparound services" or "integrated student supports." One of the most successful such programs, Boston-based City Connects, demonstrates the power of integrating strong-tie relationships into each individual student's experience.
- In some cases, integrating backward to address barriers to learning may still not be enough. Other programs, such as KIPP Through College, illustrate how some schools are integrating forward to ensure that students have the supports they need to succeed beyond high school graduation.

Notes

1. Quotes in this section of the chapter ("Love Leads the Way") are from the following source: Balian, A., Blackman, J., Brunton, J., DeGeneres, E., Gelles, J., Rief, G., . . . Yenser, A. (Writers), & Patrick, L. (Director). (2016). Serena Williams [Television series episode]. In N. Collins, M. Connelly, A. Cote, E. DeGeneres, E. Glavin, K. Hogan

Leonardo, . . . A. Zenor (Producers), *Ellen: The Ellen DeGeneres Show*. Burbank, CA: Time Telepictures Television, A Very Good Production Inc., & Telepictures Productions. Retrieved from http://gloublog.net/?p=19927

2. City Connects and Boston College Center for Optimized Student Support. (2014). The impact of City Connects: Progress report 2014. Retrieved from http://www.bc.edu/content/dam/city-connects/Publications/CityConnects_ProgressReport_2014.pdf. The remainder of this section features quotes from the authors' interview with Mary Walsh on June 13, 2017.

3. Story of our growth. City Connects. Retrieved from http://www.bc.edu/bc-web/schools/lsoe/sites/cityconnects/our-approach/story-of-our-growth.html

4. City Connects uses SSIS data for three primary purposes: "1) record-keeping at the individual and school level; 2) monitoring and evaluating the implementation of the intervention throughout the school year; and 3) conducting research on the effectiveness of the intervention." The SSIS houses key information—student reviews, individualized plans, and service referrals and providers—that allows coordinators to track student progress and continuously tweak the dosage of supports accordingly. *The impact of City Connects: Progress Report 2014*. City Connects.

5. Walsh, M. E., Madaus, G. F., Raczek, A. E., Dearing, E., Foley, C., An, C . . . Beaton, A. (2014, July). A new model for student support in high-poverty urban elementary schools: Effects on elementary and middle school academic outcomes. *American Educational Research Journal, 51,* 704–737. Retrieved from https://www.researchgate.net/profile/Mary_Walsh7/publication/276197038_A_New_Model_for_Student_Support_in_High-Poverty_Urban_Elementary_Schools_Effects_on_Elementary_and_Middle_School_Academic_Outcomes/links/57673a3b08ae1658e2f71b1e/A-New-Model-for-Student-Support-in-High-Poverty-Urban-Elementary-Schools-Effects-on-Elementary-and-Middle-School-Academic-Outcomes.pdf

6. City Connects. (2016). The impact of City Connects—Progress report 2016. Retrieved from https://www.bc.edu/content/dam/files/schools/lsoe/cityconnects/pdf/City%20Connects%20Progress%20Report%202016.pdf

7. Boston Public Schools uses the SAT to determine eligibility for advanced coursework. Teachers are thus less likely to "teach to the test," and "performance on the SAT-9 is not used by schools to make important decisions such as promotion for all students, or for teacher evaluation." Thus, concludes City Connects, "the outcomes represent more generalized academic skills." City Connects and Boston College Center for Optimized Student Support. (2014), The impact of City Connects: Progress report 2014.

8. City Connects and Boston College Center for Optimized Student Support. (2011). The impact of City Connects: Annual report 2010. Retrieved from https://www.bc.edu/content/dam/city-connects/Publications/CityConnects_AnnualReport_2010.pdf

9. Dearing, E., Walsh, M. E., Sibley, E., Lee-St. John, T., Foley, C., & Raczek, A. E. (2016). Can community and school-based supports improve the achievement of first-generation immigrant children attending high-poverty schools? *Child Development, 87*(3), 883–897. doi:10.1111/cdev.12507. Cited in City Connects. (2016). The impact of City Connects: Student outcomes—Progress report 2016. Retrieved from https://www.bc.edu/content/dam/files/schools/lsoe/cityconnects/pdf/City%20Connects%20Progress%20Report%202016.pdf

10. Here, we use the phrase "increasingly sophisticated" to describe statistical methods that are generally considered to be more effective at peeling out causal effects. These methods include those specifically designed to address selection bias, such as the

difference-in-differences (DiD) approach, which removes bias from unobserved student characteristics. For more, see Buckley, J., & Shang, Y. (2003, November). Estimating policy and program effects with observational data: The "differences-in-differences" estimator. *Practical Assessment, Research & Evaluation, 8*(24). Retrieved from http://PAREonline.net/getvn.asp?v=8&n=24. City Connects' 2016 progress report represents a good source for learning more about the methods employed by various researchers in recent studies.

11. Examples of this from history through to the present abound. For example, some Native American children were taken from their communities and sent to boarding schools where they were forced to "assimilate" into white culture. See History and culture: Boarding schools. (n.d.). Northern Plains Reservation Aid. Retrieved from http://www.nativepartnership.org/site/PageServer?pagename=airc_hist_boardingschools. Much more recently, records of the machinery of the foster system suggest that parents and guardians can be shut out of the process prematurely or altogether. See, for example, Clifford, S., & Silver-Greenberg, J. (2017, July 21). Foster care as punishment: The new reality of "Jane Crow." *New York Times*. Retrieved from https://www.nytimes.com/2017/07/21/nyregion/foster-care-nyc-jane-crow.html?hp&action=click&pgtype=Homepage&clickSource=story-heading&module=second-column-region&region=top-news&WT.nav=top-news&_r=0

12. This and following paragraphs of this section of the chapter ("Covering the Costs of Care") draw from information in the following secondary and primary sources, respectively: The impact of City Connects (2016). Student outcomes—Progress report 2016; and Bowden, A. B., Belfield, C. R., Levin, H. M., Shand, R., Wang, A., & Morales, M. (2015, July). A benefit-cost analysis of City Connects. Center for Benefit-Cost Studies of Education, Teachers College, Columbia University. Retrieved from https://static1.squarespace.com/static/583b86882e69cfc61c6c26dc/t/58cfdcba1b631bf52d377cd8/1490017468049/CityConnects.pdf

13. Bowden et al. use previous outcome evaluations of City Connects to benchmark the intervention's effect on test scores and dropout rate, including the City Connects 2014 progress report and Walsh et al. (2014), A new model for student support in high-poverty urban elementary schools. Significantly, by estimating program benefits using only two variables—test scores and high school dropout rates—the analysis may well underestimate the benefit-cost ratio, as the authors note.

14. Under the model that best fits implementation data, researchers estimated net benefits of $9,280 per student, with total costs per student ranging from $1,540 to $9,320. Bowden et al. wrote, "Sensitivity tests show that the benefit-cost ratio lies somewhere between 1 and 11.8, with a best estimate of $3.00 in benefits per dollar of cost." This range indicates that the benefit-to-cost ratio is most likely above 1—the breakeven point. The higher the ratio, the more efficient the intervention.

15. The information and un- or partially integrated approaches are unlikely to provide the same kind of support to students as a fully integrated model. When it comes to addressing student mental health issues, for instance, Darcy Gruttadaro, director of advocacy at the National Association for Mental Illness, underscored that, for children, being able to "walk down the hall and see a mental health professional" reduces barriers to care. Smith, R. (2017, April 18). Bringing psychiatrists into schools can help vulnerable kids when they need it most. St. Louis Public Radio. Retrieved from http://news.stlpublicradio.org/post/bringing-psychiatrists-schools-can-help-vulnerable-kids-when-they-need-it-most#stream/0

16. Whitman, D. (2008). *Sweating the small stuff: Inner-city schools and the new paternalism*. Washington, DC: Thomas B. Fordham Institute Press.

17. KIPP Foundation. (2013). KIPP report card 2012. Retrieved from https://issuu.com/kipp/docs/report_card_2013/9

18. According to federal accountability benchmarks, KIPP posts impressive results and outperforms neighboring schools; in some cases, it even entirely closes persistent racial and socioeconomic achievement gaps. KIPP Foundation. (2016). Results: How we measure success. Retrieved from http://www.kipp.org/results/national/#question-3:-are-our-students-progressing-and-achieving-academically. According to the organization, however, "Although KIPP students were graduating high school (95%) and enrolling in colleges (89%) more than the national average (83% and 62%, respectively), their four-year college completion (33%) was only on par with the national average (31%)." See KIPP Foundation. (2011). The promise of college completion: KIPP's early successes and challenges. Retrieved from http://www.kipp.org/wp-content/uploads/2016/09/CollegeCompletionReport.pdf

19. KIPP Foundation. (n.d.). KIPP through college. Retrieved from http://www.kipp.org/approach/kipp-through-college

20. Bermudez, C. (2017, April 17). It's bigger than teaching, it's love: How KIPP is getting students to and through college. *Education Post*. Retrieved from http://educationpost.org/its-bigger-than-teaching-its-love-how-kipp-is-getting-students-to-and-through-college

21. Ibid.

CHAPTER FOUR

Edtech That Connects

How New Technologies Can Disrupt Students' Networks

Reaching beyond Your Inherited Network

Little about Sabari Raja's early life portended a future as a rising-star educational technology CEO. Raja was born in rural India to parents without college degrees and raised on a coconut farm. She attended a traditional Indian boarding school, where academic work fostered little connection to the outside world.

But Raja happened to have an uncle who was a successful business-man. So successful, in fact, he had built a large electronics manufacturing company from scratch. For the young and precocious Raja, her uncle's story hinted at possibilities that transcended the boundaries of her life on the farm. But working in business still seemed beyond reach. "It was something to aspire for, but it wasn't the same for me," Raja said, "I was just a girl from a small rural town."[1]

Nevertheless, during summer holidays, Raja began spending time with her uncle at his factory in Bangalore, the Silicon Valley of India. By sheer luck, the commute to the factory would prove as powerful as her efforts to study the actual business. Raja recalls making that drive one morning when her uncle pointed out BioCon India. The company spanned a sprawling campus that she'd seen countless times before, but had escaped her interest until then.

"I remember him pointing out the car window and asking me, 'Do you know who started that company? Her name is Kiran Mazumdar-Shaw. She's the first female entrepreneur in India to start a biotech company.'"

For Raja, this seemingly offhand comment ushered in a world of possibilities that previously felt out of reach. "Oh my God," she recalled thinking. "A woman can actually do this! Where I had come from, it just wasn't like that." Driven by this rare glimpse into a different sort of future, Raja never looked back. After earning an engineering degree and a master's in computer science, she went on to work in Texas Instruments' Education Technology division, and acquired an MBA along the way.

Later, these experiences would find new resonance. While living in the Dallas–Fort Worth area, she became involved in engaging girls in STEM. At a meeting convened by the Dallas Chamber of Commerce to discuss ways to improve STEM outcomes, she began to realize the crux of the issue. "People around the country were gathering to have these conversations, and most often they came down to students having access to industry experts and role models," she said.

But Raja was concerned that many of these programs were prone to flawed designs. They were time-intensive, didn't always match the skills of professional mentors to student learning objectives, and tended to focus too heavily on older children. "Could we leverage technology to address these gaps?" Raja wondered. Exercising the entrepreneurial instincts that had taken root on the commute in Bangalore, Raja cofounded Nepris, a platform that beams industry professionals into classrooms over video chats to bring real-world context to curriculum. Arguably a single point of reference had changed the course of Raja's life: a woman could run a company. In a nod to her experience, Nepris departs from traditional mentorship models. "Our vision," Raja said, "has not been to forge stronger one-on-one connections." Rather, the objective of Nepris is to enable *as many connections as possible,* with the aim of integrating industry relevance into everyday learning. With this new approach, Raja hopes to open up new horizons for more students like her.

Networks as a Gateway to Opportunity

Raja's story underscores a fundamental truth about opportunity: much depends on our *inherited network*. Our inherited network is the social infrastructure into which we are born and that forms around us when we are young. Across both strong- and weak-tie dimensions, inherited networks are fundamentally bounded.

Like Raja, for instance, children born into rural families to parents who have no college education may inherit a network of family and friends employed in a limited number of jobs across a similarly limited number of industries. Inherited connections are by no means negative or bad influences. They can provide all sorts of critical supports, love, and care. And these networks can propel young people into certain careers, particularly if they hope to work in industries or functions that resemble their parents'.

But as students grow older, they may find that the reach of their inherited network is limited along the dimensions that family and neighborhoods pass down. Raja, for instance, had connections to many farmers, but only a few businesspeople. Through her weak ties, she also knew, or knew of, many men leading enterprises, but no women.

Contemplating such limitations can verge on fatalistic. Are our inherited networks simply defining our destiny from the very start?

Luckily, new innovations are defying these boundaries. As Raja's own journey illustrates, new opportunities—even from seemingly tenuous, distant connections—can come along to open new doors and perspectives. And with the rise of technology, tools like Nepris make forging these connections far more feasible and affordable.

Is Technology Disrupting Our Social Networks?

New technology alone, however, will not disrupt the limitations of inherited networks. As it turns out, some of the most popular networking technologies on the market today actually *sustain* our existing networks—rather than fundamentally disrupting them. To appreciate this distinction we must first understand two different forms of innovation: sustaining innovations and disruptive innovations.[2]

Sustaining innovations make a product or service perform better in ways that customers in the mainstream market already value. For example, Apple's consistent improvements on the iPhone mark a sustaining trajectory. To satisfy its customers, the company continues to create state-of-the-art tablets and phones, adding better and better cameras, data plans, processing speeds, and applications. Sustaining innovations serve the existing customer, just better—and usually at a marginally more expensive price. Companies pursue these sustaining innovations at the higher tiers of their markets because that is what has historically helped them succeed. By charging the highest prices to their most demanding and sophisticated customers, companies can achieve the greatest profitability.

However, by doing so, companies unwittingly open the door to disruptive innovations that take root at the bottom of the market.

Disruptive innovations create an entirely new market through the introduction of a new kind of product or service. Disruptive innovations may appear worse initially, as judged by the performance metrics that mainstream customers value. But over time, these innovations improve, in turn attracting increasingly demanding customers.

Apple's early personal computers offer a clear example of disruptive innovation. Early PCs were not nearly as powerful as the minicomputers that dominated the 1970s. But they offered distinct benefits: first, they were markedly cheaper. Apple computers sold for only $2,000 apiece compared to the quarter-million-dollar price tags on minicomputers. Moreover, they required far less expertise to operate. Only data science experts could operate minicomputers, but kids and hobbyists were able to tinker with the more rudimentary early PCs.

Unlike a sustaining innovation, PCs didn't address the next-generation needs of leading customers in existing minicomputer markets. Instead, they had other attributes—namely, affordability and accessibility—that enabled new market applications to emerge. From there, PCs improved so rapidly that they ultimately could address the needs of customers in the mainstream of the market as well. Over time, personal computer companies like Apple overtook—or *disrupted*—leading minicomputer companies like Digital Equipment Corporation (DEC). By then, Apple could offer a smaller, cheaper machine that was "good enough" for many of DEC's former customers.

All told, disruptive innovations take products or services that start off costly, centralized, and requiring particular expertise and make them widely accessible, affordable, and foolproof.

At first blush, existing social networking technologies like Facebook or LinkedIn may appear to follow this pattern of disruption. In a short time, they have radically expanded the number of friends and acquaintances in our digital Rolodexes. Connections online are far less expensive than face-to-face connections, shrinking constraints on our networks historically posed by time and distance. They are not "as good as" face-to-face connections in terms of emotional connection or allowing people to touch. But they compete on new dimensions of convenience and affordability.

But mainstream social networking sites have actually done little to disrupt the *fundamental composition* of our networks. This turns out to be the case for a couple of reasons. First, evolutionary scientists have discovered that our brains can only handle so many strong ties or friendships. Technology doesn't alter our brain's bandwidth for relationships. In other words, there are actual biological limits to how far our strong-tie personal networks can be disrupted, no matter how cheap it becomes to form and maintain those strong-tie networks from afar.[3]

But what about our weak-tie networks? Social media sites do allow users to expand the number of weaker ties and mere acquaintances they can *maintain* at a time. We may not be in close contact with many former friends or colleagues. But social networking sites make it less likely that they will leave our orbit entirely. Social networking platforms thus appear to be disrupting what's known as the *decay rate*—the rate at which we tend to fall out of touch absent reconnecting—of our existing friendships across geography and time.

But even this newfound ability to keep in touch with weak ties does not address the fundamental limitations of inherited networks. By and large, social networking sites have become repositories for our offline strong- and weak-tie connections—rather than tools to form wholly new networks. For example, according to Pew Research Center, the average Facebook user knows 93 percent of her Facebook "friends" in real life.[4] There is little to suggest that networking sites have extended the reach of those people's networks to new people whom they *might not otherwise meet.*

In short, mainstream social networking technologies have certainly disrupted how we maintain connections—and the number of geographically diverse weaker connections we can maintain at once. But by and large these offer only sustaining innovations relative to the composition of our offline networks. There is less evidence that they have disrupted how we form *new connections* in the first place or even more so, *with whom.*

Facebook founder Mark Zuckerberg has himself grappled with this pattern in recent years. As he shared in a May 2017 post, "Facebook has been focused on helping you connect with people you already know. We've built AI systems to recommend 'People You May Know.' But it might be just as important to also connect you with people you should know—mentors and people outside your circle who care about you and can provide a new source of support and inspiration."[5]

Luckily, entrepreneurs in education are starting to build tools to do just that.

New Technologies Disrupting the Limits of Inherited Networks

How might technology be a tool to transcend the limitations of students' inherited networks? This will not come about if students simply sustain their networks on platforms like Facebook and LinkedIn. Instead, students will need access to innovations that activate whole new connections that would otherwise not arise in their lives.

A small but growing market of edtech tools is bringing these connections to schools. Like all potentially disruptive innovations, these new technologies are getting their start by targeting pockets of *nonconsumption*, where students' alternative is nothing at all. In many cases, these areas of nonconsumption manifest as relationship gaps between wealthy and low-income students. As described in chapter 1, these gaps show up in all sorts of ways. Some are increasing at troubling rates along such dimensions as residential segregation, parental time, and enrichment spending. They reveal situations in which relationships are proving out of reach due to the geographic or social limitations of young people's inherited networks.

Since 2014, we've been attempting to capture any and all tools that break through these limitations and enable students to forge new connections. A free, searchable market map of tools and platforms that we've found is available online at www.christenseninstitute.org/whoyouknow.

What do these disruptive innovations look like? Some are starting to offer students more relatable, frequent guidance. Others offer engaging conversations about career opportunities and real-world examples. Still others offer new channels to academic support and motivation online. In the next sections, we provide a few examples of the entrepreneurs and models at the forefront of the field.

On-Demand Advice: Multiplying Access to Relatable Guidance

As discussed in chapter 1, many students find themselves with limited access to college guidance counseling. Short of a major overhaul in how we allocate school resources, these gaps remain an inevitable by-product of cash-strapped guidance departments. In the meantime, however, a small group of disruptive technologies that offer affordable, accessible online and blended guidance counseling are beginning to crop up.

One such effort is Student Success Agency, cofounded by two college classmates, E. J. Carrion and Michael Benko. Carrion was the first in his family to graduate from college. After college, Carrion decided to pay it forward and spent a summer working with Teach for America, helping high school guidance counselors in the Southside of Chicago. As the summer progressed, he became increasingly alarmed by the area's abysmal ratio of students to counselors—at the time approximately 1,000:1.[6]

Unsurprisingly, schools had tried to compensate for these shortages by constructing more efficient processes. The result was highly streamlined but entirely impersonal: students dutifully lined up en masse outside offices and spent no more than ten minutes with their counselor, answering the same few questions and receiving the same brochures. As one of Carrion's colleagues put it, the result amounted to little more than "drive-by counseling." Counselors were left limited time and leeway to customize advice or resources to students' particular circumstances.[7]

Where many might see despair, Carrion saw a corner of the education system ripe for innovation. Enter Student Success Agency (SSA). SSA connects high school students to their own personal online "agent" who helps guide them through the college application process. SSA's agents consist of current college students recruited from around the country. Agents are paid hourly, and typically work between five and ten hours per week, minimizing overhead costs while still providing on-demand advice and support. The SSA model hinges on pairing accessibility with accountability. Agents regularly check in—rather than merely providing "drive-by" advice—over the course of the entire school year. SSA's proprietary software tracks interactions between student and mentor, assuring student safety while collecting data on engagement, progress, and outcomes for school and parent use.

Although SSA is still in its early days, the organization's results appear promising. Some observers have estimated that the average high school student receives only thirty-eight minutes of interaction with their guidance counselor per year. Instead, students who participate in SSA spend an average of thirty-eight minutes with e-mentors *per month*.[8]

Carrion and Benko are not the only entrepreneurs expanding access to advice and support online. For example, iCouldBe is an online mentoring program founded in 2000 that brings online volunteer professionals into schools serving at-risk middle and high school students.[9] Through partnerships with large employers like AT&T, iCouldBe recruits online mentors from companies. These mentors guide students through an eighty-one-activity curriculum designed to support their academic success, postsecondary educational planning, and career planning. Mentors are not traditional mentors; in most cases, they never even meet the students in person.

Like SSA, iCouldBe does not purport to replace teachers or guidance counselors in schools, or face-to-face mentors in communities. Instead, the program views these albeit limited online relationships as critical sources of encouragement to help students through the organizations' curriculum aimed at increasing self-efficacy and preparation for twenty-first-century jobs. At the same time, interacting with online mentors offers students practice opportunities for forging and strengthening relationships in their offline lives. About one third of the curriculum explicitly emphasizes networking skills by training students in how best to leverage relationships to achieve their goals.

The model has a proven track record. Researchers from Drexel University found that iCouldBe students demonstrated an increase in decision-making abilities and self-perception of their abilities to cope in school and life. In a separate study, mentees also showed enhanced career aspirations.[10]

SSA and iCouldBe are two examples of a growing supply of online tools expanding students' access to different forms of mentorship and guidance. They effectively increase the amount of time and information on offer to students who would otherwise receive scarce minutes with a counselor.

Brief Encounters: Scaling Access to Industry Professionals

Online guidance models like Student Success Agency and iCouldBe hinge on repeated interactions with the same adult over the course of multiple semesters or even years. But some connections can occur in even shorter cycles. Brief, one-off interactions can still give students new snippets of information. This can be especially powerful when it comes to offering career exploration opportunities. Students can connect with professionals working in industries into which their existing networks offer few inroads.

Tools like Nepris bring industry professionals directly into classrooms to do just that. Similarly, other tools are combining rich project-based curriculum with outside experts. For example, the Seattle-based nonprofit Educurious offers project-based courses in which experts work with students through video chat to discuss real-world problems together.

Other companies are aiming to expose students to professionals and career guidance by crowdsourcing accurate career advice in a more highly targeted and expansive manner than chance encounters—or random Google searches—afford. For example, the Boston-based start-up Career Village addresses a fundamental information matching problem: according to Career Village, although 85 percent of low-income youth in the US use Google to search for answers to questions about how to improve academic performance, forge career paths, or select a college, the answers they find on the internet are often too confusing, too cookie-cutter, or both.

By contrast, Career Village connects high school students to a network of more than fifteen thousand industry professionals who provide tailored academic, college selection, and career advice. Career Village leverages a Q&A format to enable students to ask for advice, and crowdsources answers from those professionals to answer student queries within twenty-four hours. To date, the company has provided career advice on more than eight thousand topics to more than two-and-a-half million students.[11]

More Supports: Increasing Academic Help and Spurring Motivation

Of course, investments in relationships that help students access college guidance or career advice may do little to move the needle on outcomes without similar investments in relationships that directly support academic success.

Although individualized academic support and tutoring can have profound effects on academic performance, traditional forms of tutoring are prohibitively high cost for many schools and for most students.[12] And in most classrooms, teachers struggle to provide ongoing, reliable tutoring and academic supports to each individual student. As a result, students spend the vast majority of their time in school missing out on sustained, one-on-one academic help from adults. Most obviously, online tutoring companies are stepping into this void, by starting to offer students brief encounters with tutors and other academic supports during and after class time that students might otherwise spend working alone. By some estimates, the global K–12 online tutoring market is expected to grow more than 12 percent between 2017 and 2021.[13]

Besides a clear boom of online tutoring companies that employ or crowdsource paid tutors, other models seeking to scale tutoring keep costs low by tapping volunteer networks. For example, CNA Speaking Exchange connects native English speakers from retirement homes in the US to students learning English at CNA schools in Brazil. Students connect remotely with the seniors for brief conversations in English.[14] Like online tutoring models, these chats complement more formal, face-to-face instruction happening inside CNA's brick-and-mortar language learning centers.

Of course, educators will be quick to point out that relying on cheap or free labor may offer *more* interactions, but may threaten the quality of instruction that students typically receive through live teaching. But in some models, less skilled volunteers are providing *nonacademic* supports, such as encouragement and motivation, that can still yield academic gains.

This is precisely the idea behind another innovative effort, Granny Cloud, which beams "grannies" into an innovative school model called the School in the Cloud.[15]

The School in the Cloud is itself a disruptive innovation that emerged from an experiment conducted by theoretical physicist and professor Sugata Mitra. While working as a scientist at a Delhi computer company, Mitra was asked by his boss to research the viability of public computers. Something of a radical thinker, Mitra literally made a hole in a wall, threw a computer in it, and made it available to the illiterate Indian children growing up outside his office in the Delhi slums, where formal schooling was rarely on offer. He then sat back and watched with awe as the curious children rapidly progressed from merely moving the mouse around the screen to creating Word documents without the aid of a keyboard.

Inspired by the surprising results, Mitra began conducting more advanced experiments. Delighted to see the progress children were making, Mitra built on his original model with one key modification: a woman to act as a "grandmother" to offer encouragement as the children learned. With this human intervention—designed to encourage and motivate the students, not to "teach" or deliver any content—the children's scores on a test Mitra administered increased by 67 percent, matching those of students' in one of Delhi's high-performing schools.[16]

Granny Cloud was born. An online web of adult supports (they've moved beyond only older women, but the term "granny" stuck), Granny Cloud is part of Mitra's latest effort, Self Organized Learning Environments (SOLEs).[17] In these environments—some of which resemble brick-and-mortar schools and others of which look far more informal, like his initial hole in the wall—volunteer "grannies" Skype in to offer children a welcome dose of unconditional encouragement.

Charting a Disruptive Path Forward

For some, the idea of a virtual granny may sound beyond the pale or downright ridiculous. Many will look at tools like Granny Cloud, Nepris, or Student Success Agency with a healthy dose of doubt that technology can replace face-to-face relationships. Can we deliver the tender encouragement of a grandmotherly figure over videos, across continents? Can a video chat really replace a nurturing hug or a meaningful moment of personal advice? Can online meetings really generate the sustained supports and shared experiences that successful face-to-face, year-over-year mentorship often involves? Are tools that yield simply *more* connections or time with mentors yielding the results we care about?

These are valid concerns. But they are precisely the sorts of questions people ask when disruptive innovations are afoot. Disruptive innovations don't compete head on with existing solutions or relationships in students' lives. Rather, they offer access to groups of customers typically shut out of a mainstream opportunity or market. From there, the innovations improve over time. Apple's earliest PC computers were hardly impressive compared to the expensive and sophisticated mainframe and minicomputers that dominated the 1960s and 1970s. But Apple's early PC customers didn't care. Instead, hobbyists and children were delighted that they could afford a contraption that they could use for basic word processing and computing. Over time, Apple then shepherded the PC upmarket—improving its technology to eventually serve the needs of more demanding customers with higher processing speeds and storage volume.

Children, of course, are not widgets; their development and success hinge on more than engineering the right circuitry or software. But Apple's case illustrates the nonintuitive nature of disruptive innovation: the most crucial innovations of tomorrow may not look impressive compared to state-of-the-art products of today. Instead, by offering access and afford-ability previously unimaginable, they can eventually move upmarket to serve more demanding customers.

The same goes for technology-enabled mentoring, expert, and support systems that are beginning to expand student networks. In the present moment, these early models of online or blended interactions pale in comparison to face-to-face relationships. They are short, at times impersonal, interactions. They often connect students to people from entirely different worlds, with limited time to address those differences. It's therefore tempting to scoff at the quality of the interactions and their modest contributions to academic and nonacademic outcomes alike.

But given the gaps they are currently filling in the market, these technology-enabled interactions need not compete head on with state-of-the-art face-to-face supports. They are not attempting to deliver the same value as strong, face-to-face ties in students' lives. Instead, they promise to offer *new* connections in circumstances where the current alternative is nothing at all. They can allow students who otherwise *might never meet* an engineer or lawyer to connect with working professionals. They can fill advice gaps for those students who have shockingly limited access to college guidance in high school. They can step in to encourage and motivate students learning in isolation to persist when curiosity wavers, providing a gentle nudge to press onward.

By initially targeting those circumstances in which students struggle to access human supports, these innovative tools stand to expand and diversify students' networks—disrupting, over time, the stubborn limitations of *any* students' inherited networks.

Borrowing from the sociology literature on social capital, these technologies are tending to get their start by offering weak ties. This is particularly powerful when we recall the so-called strength of weak ties. Even relationships with less intimacy, trust, and familiarity can provide crucial, plentiful sources of new information and opportunities otherwise inaccessible through some students' immediate networks.

And like any tale of disruption, the story doesn't end there. Once new models like these take root, they may start to reshape all sorts of interactions, particularly as technology improves. Soon, for instance, using 3-D cameras or holographic imaging, students will be able to connect with mentors in ways that more closely mimic face-to-face interactions. Such technology could allow students to meet with mentors thousands of miles away in fully virtual meeting spaces.[18]

Improving Quality, Monitoring Safety

These improvements will of course need to be accompanied with vigilant privacy and safety practices. Many of these tools already perform the background checks similar to those that schools regularly perform regarding in-person visitors.

For tools like Nepris and Educurious, companies have taken pains to ensure that adults and students are never interacting online alone. Those tools that allow for one-on-one interaction also apply web filters that can monitor the content of student-adult interactions and flag any potentially inappropriate content. These filters catch risky behaviors such as sharing locations or personal information that could threaten student privacy or safety. Some have gone even further to protect students' identities. For example, iCouldBe uses avatars instead of photos to protect student privacy. As filtering technologies improve, more programs will likely move to video-based interactions and chats.

At the same time, tools can start to leverage data not just for the purposes of ensuring safety but to dive into the science of connecting to improve the *quality* of interactions. Many of the organizations we've discussed in this chapter have begun using data analytics to identify predictors of successful mentee-mentor interactions. For example, with over a decade of data on mentor and mentee interactions, iCouldBe has worked with data scientists to begin to unpack the variables (such as frequency of interaction) and communication styles among both children and adults that tend to yield the best results.

These analytics could be applied in much the same way that learning analytics can drive understanding of how students learn. As better data becomes available on interactions between students and mentors—the length and style of a mentor's advice to a student, for example—we can begin to better design online and offline interactions to accelerate the formation of trusting relationships.

Diversifying on the Basis of Similarity

These disruptions in turn stand to radically change how young people form and maintain diverse weak-tie networks. In many cases, these may remain only weak ties in students' lives. In other cases, those ties that prove most helpful or salient to a student's interests or needs could be maintained over longer periods, in time transforming into ever-stronger connections with people whom students otherwise might never have met.

Diversifying students' networks may sound all well and good. But we've all met people outside our existing networks with whom we didn't click. There's a reason, after all, that we may not have known each other in the first place. Maybe we lived worlds apart and wouldn't have had much to say to each other even if we'd met. Or maybe we wouldn't have really liked one another, resenting or fearing our differences. Recall that traditional social media has done little to expand people's offline networks to include people whom they otherwise might not meet. New tools designed to forge relationships beyond students' inherited networks will face a steep slope of difference.

This poses something of a paradox: focusing on expanding students' diversity of ties could run counter to the well-studied phenomenon of homophily. Birds of a feather flock together: people trust others who are *like them*. Given that similarity breeds connection, how much can we realistically hope that students and adults from different worlds—professionally, geographically, or culturally—could start to forge productive connections, especially in the course of a brief, online encounter?

To resolve this conundrum, we can look to an age-old source of truth: beer advertising. In April 2017, savvy executives at Heineken took advantage of the political divisiveness sweeping much of the Western world. Europe was reeling in post-Brexit chaos, and France was teetering on the eve of a heated presidential election. And in the US, political debates about the direction of the country had reached a fever pitch as president Donald Trump's first one hundred days were nearing their close.[19]

Capitalizing on the tensions of the moment, Heineken released a video titled "An Experiment: Worlds Apart." In the video, regular people with wholly opposing views on everything from climate change to gender politics were brought together. As the film starts rolling, pairs of strangers meet in an abandoned warehouse and receive instructions. First, they must share five things about themselves and identify three things they have in common. Then they are told to work on a project together, building what turns out to be a rudimentary bar. After that, each pair must watch video interviews of one another expressing their political viewpoints. Only then is it revealed that the individuals who have started to get to know one another hold diametrically opposing views on divisive political issues like the environment and gender.

They are then offered the chance to sit down to discuss their differences—of course, you guessed it, over a beer. Each pair accepts the opportunity. By the end, climate deniers are hugging environmentalists and agreeing it would be fun to engage in healthy debate. A man opposed to transgender rights is exchanging phone numbers with a transgender woman, hoping to stay in touch.

No one's point of view has taken a complete 180 in the short time they've known one another. The video is not so much about changing people's minds or even necessarily eliminating bias. The pairs are, for the most part, agreeing to disagree. But they are doing so with a hint of respect and a smile grounded in some sort of shared humanity.

Of course, Heineken would like you to come away convinced that beer is the single ingredient that can lubricate the social tensions plaguing the twenty-first century. All we need to weave our polarized societies back together is to belly up to a bar to share a cold beer with strangers, right?

But beyond that not-so-subtle message, the brilliance of the ad is that it captures the power of harnessing—rather than abandoning—the phenomenon of homophily even in circumstances of profound difference. Seemingly unlike people *can* connect—even if they don't agree on everything or bring the same life experiences to the table. But breeding new connections that engender even a modicum of trust requires shedding light on shared experiences, tastes, or characteristics. And oftentimes, these get lost. Without prompts or projects that require collaboration—such as sharing five things about yourself or constructing a makeshift bar from scratch, to name a few—similarities between strangers can remain concealed behind more visible traits.

Designing Tools with Homophily in Mind

For anyone steeped in the literature on effective mentorship, Heineken's message is hardly new: establishing trust between mentors and mentees has long been emphasized in the youth development world. Absent protocols and processes that establish trust, connecting young people with adults—face-to-face or digitally—risks engaging in what we've heard Janice McKenzie-Crayton, a longtime crusader in the mentorship world, call "cymbal mentoring": crashing a mentor and mentee together like two cymbals in a marching band, harboring some blind hope that a relationship sticks.

In fact, that hope-for-the-best approach can have dire consequences. Young people who experience negative or curtailed mentoring relationships show marked *decreases* in their sense of self-worth and academic ability.[20]

Emerging technology tools that expand students' access to new weak-tie connections could yield equally harmful and counterproductive results. Without attention to the right design, they risk digitally "crashing" adults and young people from different backgrounds together without scaffolds and supports to nurture trust. Tools, after all, are just platforms. They could either function as conduits for new, positive interactions *or* as forums where misunderstanding and discrimination play out in spades. The risk, then, of not addressing difference and discrimination head on is that young people would in turn find themselves facing an even worse outlook (by the sheer volume of interactions made possible through new tools) than they did in a less networked world.

To mitigate these risks, edtech tools must embrace homophily by surfacing similarities between people even in digital environments. They must also take pains to address head on the ways that implicit bias could creep into interactions between students and adults from different backgrounds. What might this look like?

For starters, the process of matching students and adults can take similarity into consideration. Platforms like iCouldBe, for instance, allow students to pick their mentors based on shared careers, hobbies, and interests. Other tools offer conversation protocols designed to surface similarities among participants. For example, in a pilot to help third-graders forge relationships across different cultures and geographies, Educurious partnered with the nonprofit Empatico.org to allow students to work on projects through virtual environments. To begin these projects, students were instructed to engage in conversations that produce "me-too moments." Pairs begin describing themselves to one another until they are able to say "me too." A me-too conversation might go something like this:

DAN: Hello, my name is Daniel.
JULIA: Hi, I'm Julia. [She can't say "me too" because her name isn't Daniel.]
DAN: My middle name is Thomas.
JULIA: My middle name is Frances. [Still not me too.]
DAN: I was named after my great-grandfather.
JULIA: Me too!—Francis was my grandfather's middle name.

A me-too moment represents a jumping-off point for nurturing empathy and trust. Small moments like these may seem frivolous. They are, after all, just a sliver of a person's whole identity. But they are important footholds. Absent such designs, tools that might otherwise chart a disruptive course risk merely reinforcing existing inherited networks by organizing new relationships along the usual dimensions—race, culture, or creed—or by crashing people together despite their apparent, unassailable differences and producing negative interactions.

Of course, surfacing similarity is only one crucial design consideration if tools are aiming to create new, positive connections in young people's lives. But new tools designed to fundamentally expand students' networks will likely need to embrace other approaches, aimed at surfacing and addressing implicit bias and setting the stage for interactions grounded in mutual respect for one another's background and culture.[21]

A New Design for Schools

Innovative technologies could be game-changing. Tools like those described in this chapter could allow schools to invest meaningfully—and at an affordable price tag—in their students' networks. The shifts that new technologies offer are not without risk. But given the current landscape of opportunity gaps, these tools' upside potential is enormous. Limited inherited networks and mere chance encounters need no longer spell students' fate. Powerful webs of technology-enabled connections that diversify young people's networks are increasingly within reach.

Paired with integrated supports described in the previous chapter, schools have at their fingertips both innovative architectures to integrate social supports, and disruptive tools to expand students' social capital. If schools are truly society's "great equalizer," they must pick up this mantle and redesign themselves to better function as both caring and networking hubs. They must design themselves to be far-reaching—rather than merely embryonic—communities. In our next chapter, we explore several schools that are doing just that.

KEY TAKEAWAYS

- An individual's inherited network is the social infrastructure into which she is born and that forms around her as the natural outcome of inherited circumstances.
- Inherited networks are bounded and impose limits on life outcomes for all young people, but particularly threaten to limit social mobility

for students from low-income backgrounds. Closing the opportunity gap requires disrupting the limitations of inherited networks.

- Fortunately, a powerful supply of technology-enabled tools that can diversify young people's networks is increasingly within reach. These tools are targeting pockets of the education system that have long gone neglected: widespread access to industry experts in the real world; frequent access to college guidance and support; and ongoing, tailored academic support and encouragement for individual students.

- To forge these connections, innovations that stand to increase students' social capital can leverage the concept of homophily to diversify on the basis of similarity. This could increase the likelihood that new relationships will flourish on the foundation of mutual respect and trust.

Notes

1. Author interview with Sabari Raja, November 28, 2016. All subsequent quotes from Raja are also from this interview.
2. Definitions and examples of sustaining and disruptive innovation can be found in Christensen, C., & Raynor, M. (2013). *The innovator's solution: Creating and sustaining successful growth.* Boston, MA: Harvard Business Review Press.
3. Dunbar, R. I. (1998). The social brain hypothesis. *Evolutionary Anthropology, 9*(10), 178–190. doi:10.1002/(SICI)1520–6505(1998)6:5<178::AID-EVAN5>3.0.CO;2–8; Pollet, T. V., Roberts, S. G., & Dunbar, R. I. (2011). Use of social network sites and instant messaging does not lead to increased offline social network size, or to emotionally closer relationships with offline network members. *Cyberpsychology, Behavior, and Social Networking, 14,* 253–258. doi:10.1089/cyber.2010.0161
4. Hampton, K., Goulet, L. S., Rainie, L., & Purcell, K. (2011). Social networking sites and our lives. *Pew Internet & American Life Project, 16,* 1–85. Retrieved from http://pewinternet.org/Reports/2011/Technology-and-social-networks.aspx
5. Victor, R. (2017, May 22). Zuckerberg: Facebook looking at connecting you with "people you should know." *MarketWatch.* Retrieved from https://www.marketwatch.com/story/zuckerberg-facebook-looking-at-connecting-you-with-people-you-should-know-2017-05-22
6. Author interview with E. J. Carrion, May 15, 2015.
7. Collegiate Entrepreneurs' Organization. (2014, June 10). *EJ Carrion—2014 CEO National Conference Emcee – Interview* [Video file]. Retrieved from https://www.youtube.com/watch?v=y0dWtoQnHgk
8. Author email communication with E. J. Carrion, January 2018.
9. Author interview with iCouldBe executive director Kate Schrauth, April 29, 2015.

10. Linnehan, F., DiRenzo, M. S., Shao, P., & Rosenberg, W. L. (2010). A moderated mediation model of e-mentoring. *Journal of Vocational Behavior 76,* 292–305. doi: 10.1016/j.jvb.2009.10.003; DiRenzo, M. S., Weer, C. H., & Linnehan, F. (2013). Protégé career aspirations: The influence of formal e-mentor networks and family-based role models. *Journal of Vocational Behavior, 83*(1), 41–50. doi:10.1016/j.jvb.2013.02.007

11. Career Village (n.d.). About. Retrieved from https://www.careervillage.org/about

12. Bloom, B. S. (1984). The 2 sigma problem: The search for methods of group instruction as effective as one-to-one tutoring. *Educational Researcher, 13*(6), 4–16. doi:10.3102/0013189X013006004

13. Technavio. (2016). *Global K–12 online tutoring market 2017–2021.* Retrieved from https://www.reportbuyer.com/product/4594288/

14. Chats last for eleven minutes and are uploaded to a private YouTube channel for teacher evaluation. CNA. (n.d.). Speaking Exchange. Retrieved from https://www.cna .com.br/sobre-cna/exchange

15. Cadwalladr, C. (2015, August 2). The "granny cloud": The network of volunteers helping poorer children learn. *Guardian.* Retrieved from https://www.theguardian .com/education/2015/aug/02/sugata-mitra-school-in-the-cloud

16. Ibid.

17. See School in the Cloud. (n.d.). Global SOLEs. Retrieved from https://www .theschoolinthecloud.org/globalsolesintro

18. Research suggests that the richer the modality of communication, the more capable we are of forming empathy and emotion, even when the interaction is mediated by technology. See Sherman, L. E., Michikyan, M., & Greenfield, P. M. (2013). The effects of text, audio, video, and in-person communication on bonding between friends. *Cyberpsychology: Journal of Psychosocial Research on Cyberspace, 7*(2), article 3. doi:10.5817/ CP2013-2-3

19. Berkowitz, J. (2017, April 26). Heineken just put out the antidote to that Pepsi Kendall Jenner ad. *Fast Company.* Retrieved from https://www.fastcompany.com/40412848/ heineken-just-put-out-the-antidote-to-that-pepsi-kendall-jenner-ad

20. Schwartz, S. E., Lowe, S. R., & Rhodes, J. E. (2012). Mentoring relationships and adolescent self-esteem. *Prevention Researcher, 19*(2), 17–20. Retrieved from https://www .ncbi.nlm.nih.gov/pmc/articles/PMC3873158

21. Studies of the sharing economy have begun to explore methods of combating bias and discrimination that arise in online communities and marketplaces. This will be a crucial research and policy topic as more tools like those in this chapter scale. For example, see Abrahao, B., Parigi, P., Gupta, A., & Cook, K. S. (2017). Reputation offsets trust judgments based on social biases among Airbnb users. *Proceedings of the National Academy of Sciences, 114*(37), 9848–9853. doi:10.1073/pnas.1604234114

CHAPTER FIVE

Making Space for Relationships

Redesigning School as a Caring and Networking Hub

"How Do I Slot In?"

We've been sharing the ideas in this book for a number of years. More often than not, our conversations prompt people to reminisce about the relationships that have shaped their lives. In fact, it's proven to be a great way to break the ice and move beyond small talk. At other times, however, we are reminded of just how far the current system has to go. One particular interaction back in 2015 has stuck with us.

At an event in Boston hosted by the public radio station WGBH, Julia had the chance to sit on a panel discussion about expanding STEM pathways for students. The panel covered many of the usual methods for improving STEM that tend to surface at education conferences. Panelists discussed better teacher recruitment and preparation, hands-on learning experiences, and digital content tools (to name a few).

Given chronic shortages in STEM teachers, it seemed like a perfect chance to note the potential to bring more industry experts to bear in STEM classrooms. Citing tools like Nepris and Educurious, described in chapter 4, Julia explained how students could enjoy science alongside real-life scientists. But when it came time for the Q&A, one parent in the audience pressed the panel on how exactly this would work.

In addition to being a mother to a kindergartener, she was a scientist. An accomplished archaeologist and geophysicist, to be exact. She was passionate about science education, had a background in building curriculum, and was actively seeking to get involved in her daughter's school. But when she'd met with administrators and the local school board, the response had been tepid. "I've said I'd like to come in . . . I'll bring equipment, like my ground-penetrating radar, and we can do physics. I'll bring my trowel, and we can excavate," she said. "But the feedback I've gotten is, 'Well, we don't really have time for you to be involved.'" The mother acknowledged that she understood the demands that teachers faced, and communicated that she was willing to be flexible. "The thing is, I'm happy to fit in," she had told them. "You can tell me what you need." But that flexibility and willingness hadn't made a difference. "My question," she said to the panel, "is how can I slot in?"

Her language was apt. In theory, bringing outside experts, mentors, or community agencies to bear in schools all sounds well and good. And conceptually, the additional help ought to be a boon to teachers and students alike. But in reality, few "slots" exist in the current architecture of K–12 schools to accommodate the outside world—or the people in it.

The Current Architecture Closing Off School

These kinds of structural limitations are common in traditional school design. In fact, many well-intended education policies inadvertently turn schools inside, rather than out. For example, most schools award academic credit based on students' time spent literally *inside* school—dubbed seat-time. This prevents most students from earning academic credit for learning experiences with adults and mentors out in their communities. School security policies, meanwhile, often keep students from leaving their school's physical campus. Likewise, in digital environments, student privacy and safety policies can limit students to impersonal anonymous or asynchronous interactions with online mentors. And with annual high-stakes tests looming each spring, K–12 schools face incredible pressure to deliver standards-aligned content on a rigid schedule. To meet these standards as efficiently as possible, centralized curriculum decisions often box educators into drawing from prefabricated content in textbooks, rather than relying on knowledge from an array of industry experts in a given subject or field.

Although policies like these are all defensible, they reinforce the closed-off community that makes up most schools. As the mother-geophysicist's thwarted efforts suggest, within this self-contained and tightly scheduled architecture, even the most willing volunteers (and some of the strongest ties in children's lives) can't seem to fit in.

If we consider the forces operating on the education system, this should hardly come as a surprise. Flexibility rarely comes naturally to bureaucracies. Schools tend to rely on standardized processes that are, by default, insensitive to unique circumstances or new resources. Luckily, however, innovations tend to find fault lines in entrenched systems, igniting forces that can eventually disrupt the staid, fixed structures guiding schools. And from there, schools can evolve to a new architecture that includes many "slots" through which students connect with outside mentors and experts. Those outsiders may be the community-based organizations or virtual mentors described in the previous chapters. They may also be geophysicists, parents, or even—as the case may be—both.

Innovations Reshaping School Architecture

To envision how this new architecture might unfold, we need to understand the new instructional models emerging in K–12 schools—and how they are starting to give rise to a new set of "slots" through which students can access learning. Then we can consider how this architecture stands to help schools tackle relationship gaps writ large.

Schools, it turns out, are no strangers to disruptive innovation. The last two decades have witnessed the rise of online learning as a whole new modality for delivering academic instruction. Online learning has in some cases supplemented, and in others entirely displaced, traditional instructional models grounded in textbooks and lecture-style teaching.

Our colleagues Clay Christensen, Michael Horn, and Curtis Johnson chronicled the rise of online learning in their 2008 book, *Disrupting Class.* Like other disruptive innovations, such as Apple's earliest personal computers, online learning got its start targeting pockets of nonconsumption, where students were historically unable to access learning. These included subject areas in which schools were struggling to offer coursework, such as

Advanced Placement, credit recovery, and elective language and honors courses. Before the advent of online courses, for many schools, these subjects had proved too costly to hire full-time staff to teach.[1]

Early online courses were rudimentary at best. They often consisted of static content or limited interactions with online instructors. They could hardly compete with the dynamism of courses taught face-to-face. But by targeting nonconsumption, they instead competed against circumstances where students' alternative was nothing at all.

In the years since its emergence, however, online learning has improved significantly, much as Christensen, Horn, and Johnson predicted. Edtech tools now leverage many of the advances reshaping our twenty-first-century lives, such as elaborate algorithms, video and live chat functionalities, and sophisticated data analytics. Although by no means perfect for all learners or all circumstances, online learning has become "good enough" to make its way into core academic subjects like math and English.

Although some students now attend fully virtual schools from home, most students still attend traditional brick-and-mortar settings. Rather than displacing the physical schoolhouse, by and large online learning has taken the form of *blended learning*.[2] In blended models, students learn partly online and partly in brick-and-mortar, face-to-face settings. By some estimates, over 75 percent of school districts presently offer at least some form of blended learning.[3]

As a disruptive force, online learning presents an inroad to breaking open the constraints of traditional monolithic instructional models. To better understand how this evolution might occur, and how new "slots" for relationships and networks can emerge, we first must grasp the business models of schools and content providers behind this transition.

Transitioning away from Batch-Processing Students

Many teachers do their best to differentiate learning experiences to meet the needs of individual students. But our traditional school model is organized around educating age-based cohorts of young people. At its worst, this model treats children as batches of "widgets." Translated into business terms, most schools employ what's known as a *value-adding process (VAP)* model, much like that of a manufacturing company.[4]

VAP entities bring inputs of materials into one end of the premises, transform them by "adding value," and then deliver higher-value products to customers at the other end. By policy, schools are charged with "adding value" to young people by delivering content and skills to meet standardized goals. Many adopt standardized curricula through textbook companies and deliver content en masse to batches of students.

VAP business models emerge in circumstances where providers can theoretically deliver value predictably through standardized processes. But because of variable student needs, variable family resources, and variable school and educator quality, the traditional VAP school model is a far cry from a finely tuned manufacturing facility. In many cases, schools advance students from one grade to the next even if they have not mastered the skills and acquired the knowledge necessary for success in higher grades. Some students succeed, but many do not. Instead, as gaps in their understanding inevitably accumulate, they risk falling further and further behind.[5]

Innovations in online learning, however, are beginning to make a dent in the VAP model that dominates our school system. Although many online courses are still procured and delivered in this VAP structure at schools (pushing students through online coursework in much the same manner as traditional face-to-face courses), online "modules" of instruction are increasingly doled out flexibly to different students, at different times, in combination with face-to-face instruction. Although many curriculum providers still sell full courses' worth of material (as would a traditional textbook provider), schools are starting to mix and match content from a variety of providers. Schools are also pairing provider offerings with their own teacher-created online content to better meet their students' individual needs or interests.

The rise of online courses marked a first phase of disruptive innovation relative to traditional classes. But as *Disrupting Class* predicted, online learning offerings will over time likely give rise to a second phase of disruption. This phase will yield a new business model that will overtake schools' current VAP approach to acquiring curriculum and delivering instruction: a *facilitated network*. In a facilitated network model, customers exchange with one another. Rather than making money by adding value to discrete products in an assembly line (VAP), facilitated networks prosper by enabling connections between users.[6]

For example, the online auction site eBay functions as a facilitated network. The company doesn't produce any goods. Rather, it enables millions of users to buy and sell goods among themselves in a reliable, safe manner. By acting as a facilitator, eBay unlocks channels—or *slots*—through which sellers can enter the marketplace to find willing buyers for everything from a $14.83 broken laser pointer (rumored to be the first item ever sold on the website) to a $168 million Gigayacht (the most expensive item ever sold, at least as of 2017).

For schools, moving from a VAP to a facilitated network model would mean opening up varied slots both for online curriculum and lessons and for offline experiences and projects. In such a model, learning experiences or modules need not come from a single course provider (such as a textbook company or online course company). Nor must content be taught by a single teacher to many students simultaneously. And all students need not access the same content at all. Instead, schools making purchasing decisions in such a marketplace could increasingly integrate numerous learning or tutoring modules and experiences from a suite of providers. And as software tools emerge that allow teachers to create content ever more easily, students and teachers alike could also contribute to the marketplace, while enjoying unprecedented flexibility in where they access learning.

Going Online to Get Offline

Presently, this second phase of disruption is occurring only at the very edges of the education market. No single platform—an eBay for learning—exists. But a subset of schools are beginning to move beyond single, cohort-based courses, to mix and match content and tutoring tools from a variety of online providers in order to better customize instruction. In turn, as schools start to pull in a range of online learning tools, a range of powerful *offline* experiences—such as collaborative projects, one-on-one coaching and tutoring, and out-of-school learning—are emerging in parallel.[7]

It is these tectonic shifts that stand to open up new slots for a variety of online and offline relationships to permeate schools.

For example, within the walls of the California-based Summit Public Schools, students cover core content knowledge working online from a "playlist" consisting of a mix of teacher-created lessons and third-party content from providers like Khan Academy.[8] The playlist lives on the Summit Learning Platform, developed in partnership with Facebook engineers. With immediate, near-real-time feedback from analytics coming through the back end of the playlist, Summit teachers can identify areas where students are struggling, and flex face-to-face time for small-group or one-on-one instruction as needed.

Online learning is the backbone of Summit's playlist model, but it is certainly not the school's only component. In fact, in addition to opening up more room for personalized face-to-face instruction, it has unlocked a range of offline *experiences*: 70 percent of a student's grade depends on her perform-ance on numerous team projects, in which students develop higher-order skills such as problem solving and creative thinking. They might, for instance, use mathematical modeling to forecast stock market growth, or develop products designed to mitigate heat exhaustion in athletes.[9]

In addition to a mix of online and offline learning *within* school, Summit also offers opportunities for students to connect with the world *outside* the classroom. Every year, Summit students spend a total of eight weeks on "expeditions" that run the gamut from internships to wilderness travel. Although Summit tasks a number of its full-time teachers with overseeing some of these experiences, it also works with a range of guest instructors to run two-week courses for which students receive elective credit. These experiences are heavily vetted for both quality and student safety. Instructors range from industry experts to local nonprofit leaders to professional tutors.[10]

Projects, internships, and electives, of course, are available at even the most traditional of schools. But these opportunities often exist in a one-off manner—rather than as integrated components of a whole-school model that makes such experiences a core aspect of each student's journey. Summit's deliberate architecture is opening up a range of slots for projects and out-of-school learning that most schools struggle to deliver at scale, to each and every student.[11]

Awarding Credit for Real-World Experiences

Summit is hardly the only school that has ridden the wave of online learning to develop a more open, networked architecture of school. On the other side of the country, in a town that couldn't feel farther from Summit's Silicon Valley corridor, another innovative model has taken root.

The Virtual Learning Academy Charter School (VLACS) is a fully virtual, public middle and high school headquartered in Exeter, New Hampshire. At VLACS, students can earn credit through five "pathways." VLACS takes out-of-school learning a step further than Summit, awarding core academic credit for some out-of-school activities.

VLACS has long been a small but crucial national experiment in how to scale what are often referred to as *competency-based approaches,* which are discussed in great detail in chapter 7. In a competency-based model, students advance upon mastery, rather than based on a class- or school-wide schedule. This means that in a single class, students might be working through a wide variety of learning objectives spanning various levels. In other words, it does away with a single "course" that all students take at once.

To that end, VLACS offers students flexibly paced learning modules broken down to the grain size of the competency, rather than an entire course. But their latest model scales flexibility in both pace *and path*: VLACS students can learn not just through online modules but also through projects, experiences in their communities, team-based activities, or dual enrollment in local colleges. "Experiences" are in many ways more extensive versions of Summit's "expeditions": students can, for example, serve in an internship, participate in service learning, or travel.[12] Experiences happen out in the real world. But unlike at Summit, these real-world experiences are treated as core academic credit-bearing activities in the same way that online or project-based learning modules are.

Moreover, in defiance of the singular, predefined path that most schools offer, VLACS students can mix and match content and experiences from these five pathways, at their own pace, to customize a school experience that fits their needs and interests. VLACS's founder Steve Kossakoski is careful to note that this mix of options is just that—a mix. "It's pretty safe to assume that a student will not master every competency in Algebra I during a semester-long internship," he said. "However, during an internship, a student may master two Algebra competencies and a science competency and come away with an understanding of how important these disciplines are in the real world."[13]

Opening Up to Out-of-School Learning

New tech-enabled school models like VLACS and Summit are still evolving. But they are showing how the disruptive force of online learning can unlock a facilitated network model of content and experiences that allows for far greater flexibility in how students learn. Flexibility, in turn, has resulted in a budding emphasis in schools like VLACS and Summit on treating projects and experiences as core conduits of learning and development, rather than as "nice-to-have" curricular supplements. As the slots through which learning can occur multiply, these new pathways are starting to turn schools inside out.

It bears noting that Summit and VLACS are by no means the first school models to test the waters of integrating in-school and out-of-school experiences. Before online learning had really taken off, Big Picture Learning—a nonprofit founded in 1995 in Providence, Rhode Island—allowed students to spend a significant portion of the school year learning through student interest–driven internships in their communities.

To this day, Big Picture Learning schools source internships through various channels—parents and their networks, partnerships with local businesses, educator networks, and more. Over the course of their internships, students are assessed through public displays, presentations, and exhibitions of learning against the real-world standards of a project. These exhibitions take place in a community of internship-site mentors, teachers (which Big Picture Learning calls "advisors"), peers, and parents.

Suffice it to say, more than most schools today, Big Picture Learning would have understood how to collaborate with willing scientists such as a geophysicist mother. Since its inception, Big Picture Learning has treated the community as a key slot in the architecture of its schools. Yet outside Big Picture Learning's seventy-plus school network in the US (and many more internationally), this open, real-world approach can prove challenging to scale. This comes as no surprise. Traditional schools' VAP batch-processing models of instruction, by their very design, tend to reward centralized, standardized approaches to the detriment of student-centered and community-based approaches. Big Picture Learning's approach simply does not square with the traditional system's value proposition and the architecture that supports it.

The tide of the traditional system's architecture, however, is turning. Examples like Summit and VLACS show how schools are pursuing facilitated network–like learning models that mix and match online content with offline learning experiences. These innovations are opening up the possibility of new pathways for learning both inside and outside school as we know it.

Can Innovations in *Learning* and *Connecting* Work Together?

Returning to the topic of students' networks, these developments beg some important questions: Do such changes in how students *learn* stand to reshape how students *connect*? Can innovations that expand students' access to relationships evolve *alongside* the online and blended learning innovations that are fundamentally reshaping school designs?

The answer is, it depends.

Shifting to online learning could radically open up the architecture of school to strengthen and expand students' networks. But some schools have focused heavily on online learning to the *detriment* of relationships. In such cases, online learning has become what journalist Zoe Kirsch aptly dubbed the "big shortcut."[14] Using online modules, particularly for credit recovery, schools have effectively parked struggling students in front of computers, clicking them through online units of instruction. In these models, schools often use learning labs that confine students to real or effective cubicles. Online learning under these conditions may still offer crucial flexibility absent in traditional schools, but it diminishes human interaction.

In other words, in some corners of the education system, online learning has proven to be an alluringly cheap means to deliver the worst of factory-like VAP-model instruction. As Kirsch chronicled, in cases like credit recovery, policy may be the culprit. Policies focused on graduating students on time can be grossly misaligned with high-quality learning, much less connecting. All of this poses the danger of online options isolating students even further than a traditional school model, exacerbating network gaps rather than closing them.

But looking ahead, an influx of online curriculum does not have to spell the end of human interaction. Adopting online modules need not mean that students are sitting in real or virtual corners wearing headphones with their eyes glued to computer screens. Instead, as Summit and VLACS demonstrate, blended and online learning models can actually *open up* critical time and space for teachers to get to know their students better, and for students to engage more regularly with experts and mentors beyond the four walls of their school. Such a combination can increase both the *quantity* and the *quality* of students' connections.

Strengthening Teacher-Student Ties

The relationship between a student and a teacher can be sacred. Reminiscing on our school days, most of us can recall teachers who inspired us to be the best version of ourselves. Still, finding time to invest regularly in close relationships with *each and every* student can prove difficult, particularly in models that resist customization.

But new school models that embrace flexible learning pathways could be designed to strengthen the ties between teachers and students.[15] We've already touched on how this works at Summit, where teachers have more time to instruct small groups or individual students. But in addition to instructional supports, Summit's model also focuses on deep mentoring relationships between students and teachers beyond core academic class time. All students are assigned a mentor teacher with whom they meet weekly during dedicated "Mentor Time." Students work closely with their mentors on everything from goal setting to college readiness to personal growth. Many students remain with the same mentor year over year. According to 2016 estimates, these adults manage to spend an incredible *minimum* of two hundred hours per year coaching, mentoring, and simply getting to know individual students and their families.[16]

And despite being fully virtual, relationships likewise sit at the center of VLACS's model as well. Echoing Kirsch's findings, Kossakoski said in a 2016 interview, "When you think about virtual education, it's often more about efficiency and getting more students through than it is about relationships."[17] But Kossakoski wanted to build VLACS in a way that bucked that trend. For example, VLACS assessments hinge on one-on-one discussions between teachers and students—a rare model in the virtual learning space, much less in brick-and-mortar schools. "It's very unusual for a school to say that every student has a 20- to 30-minute discussion about an academic concept with their instructor one-on-one, and then to be able to say that happens in a full-credit course, between 8 and 12 times," he said. In Kossakoski's opinion, the approach begets better connections *and* assessments. "In addition to building that relationship, there's also the ability to have deep discussions about the concepts they're working on, which lends another level of authenticity to it."[18]

And at Big Picture Learning, even though students spend significant time outside school with nonteacher mentors, it is teachers who anchor the student experience. For all four years of high school, each Big Picture Learning student is part of a small learning community of fifteen students called an advisory. Advisory is often described as a "second family" by students, within which they build "close personal relationships that last a lifetime."[19] If that sounds like a marketing ploy, it's worth noting that data from a subset of Big Picture Learning schools support these claims: in that sample, 96 percent of teacher-advisors were in direct or indirect contact with their students two years after graduation.[20]

Other Ties in Students' Lives

All three of these models show the promise of shifting the structure of school to deliberately strengthen ties between students and teachers. However, schools face a lurking, inconvenient truth: when it comes to curing opportunity gaps, teacher-student relationships are not enough. As we've noted throughout this book, study after study suggests that students desperately need a *web* of relationships. Acknowledging the mix of strong and weak ties that help everyone get by and get ahead in life, we should hardly expect dedicated teachers to serve as the sole source of social capital that schools provide to their students. Doing so sells teachers and students short.

Luckily, the same new school designs that can strengthen teacher-student connections could also expand students' weaker-tie networks in their communities and beyond. And for that to occur, innovations in *connecting* will need to evolve alongside innovations in *learning*.

The Next Phase of Schools: Walled Gardens for Learning and Connecting

How might this evolution ensue? Looking to the shifts occurring at the frontiers of school innovation offers some clues. First, it's worth noting that despite their efforts to break open the traditional VAP batch-processing model of instruction, neither Summit nor VLACS has made the full flip to a facilitated network of content, and even less so to a facilitated network of out-of-school connections and experiences. Students at these schools do not enjoy the enormous flexibility of options that, say, eBay shoppers looking to decorate their home or update their closet do—at least not yet. Even though both models are diversifying the range of learning experiences and connections students can access, the supply of those options still remains relatively narrow.

Instead, both Summit and VLACS essentially function today as *walled gardens*—more like individual "stores" that have significantly expanded their own array of products than as full-fledged open marketplaces through which any willing expert like the devoted geophysicist can walk in the door (or online portal) at either school.

Both schools use a healthy mix of third-party online content and various learning modalities. But absent an existing robust marketplace of projects, expeditions, and experiences, schools like Summit and VLACS must carefully *curate* and in some cases even create many of these learning experiences themselves. Put differently, architecturally speaking, the new slots multiplying across these instructional models are not fully open or modular interfaces into which a variety of providers or new relationships might plug in. Instead, they remain heavily controlled by the school itself (see Figure 5.1).

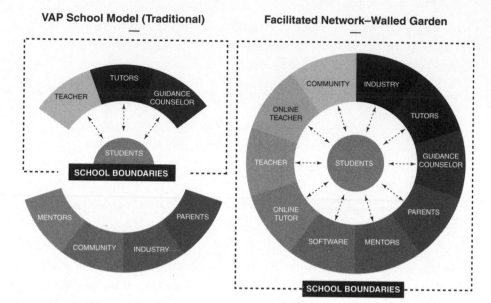

Figure 5.1 Moving to a Walled Garden

This should not come as a surprise if we recall the concepts of interdependence and modularity described in chapter 2. Industries often evolve from interdependent architectures—in which providers or, in this case, schools, control the entire creation of a product or service—to modular ones, in which a range of players can provide reliable subcomponent parts. For example, as the performance of its mainframe computers improved, IBM moved gradually from a highly integrated production model to a modular one. Still, for many years it continued to control the interfaces against which it outsourced production. Only later, and in a piecemeal fashion, did the introduction of the Mainframe 360 allow for peripherals like printers and readers to become truly modular. This, in turn, gave rise to an entire market of suppliers that specialized in building these specific devices.[21]

Innovations in connecting and learning beyond traditional school boundaries are still in their early days. Schools looking to expand students' opportunities and connections beyond the traditional classroom have effectively had to integrate across the interface that historically separated school and the outside word—and the mentors, experts, and parents in it.

And as they build out additional slots for connections and experiences, schools like Summit and VLACS will likely remain focused on improving performance. For some, this will mean increasing the reliability and quality of curriculum along traditional measures, such as increasing test scores. For others, this may mean improving learning and connecting along other measures—for example, bolstering students' noncognitive skills or increasing access to high-quality guidance. For all schools, tight control will be especially crucial for figuring out how best to monitor student privacy and safety, while loosening access to more adults. This last component will be discussed further in chapter 7.

The need to control various and sundry aspects of school design will persist until a more reliable understanding of what works, for which students, in which circumstances can better define the exact contours of various "slots." From there, emerging tools that facilitate myriad, even more diverse connections stand to rapidly grow just as specialized suppliers did in the computing market.

Tools to Curate Walled Gardens

Consistent with this current stage of innovation, it's hardly surprising that we're witnessing the rise of tools that could support highly curated walled-garden approaches to a new school architecture.

In fact, well into its second decade, Big Picture Learning decided to build a tool called ImBlaze. ImBlaze is a software tool designed to help other schools coordinate internship opportunities. It allows schools, districts, and regions to build their own dynamic database of internships. True to Big Picture Learning's emphasis on student-centered learning, students themselves populate the database with connections in their own lives and through outreach to local businesses that pique their interest. From there, the tool allows educators and administrators to verify the quality of various opportunities and track a student's journey to and through the internship experience, including when the student checks in or out of the internship site. Schools that have been doing this for decades now have a new tool at their disposal that allows them to ensure in real time that both students and internship hosts are having a valued experience. Schools that are only beginning to explore out-of-school learning have a tool to begin to organize those efforts.

Like many of the still-evolving learning tools we've discussed, ImBlaze adheres to the walled-garden approach: it uses a VAP business model to license software that allows schools to build their own proprietary market of internship opportunities.

Over time, however, as these opportunities start to scale, we can imagine a tool with an architecture similar to that of ImBlaze that begins to look less like a single school's "database" and more like an open marketplace where community-based learning experiences, students, and schools can connect directly.

The nature of these opportunities will vary by geography. In circumstances where schools can tap local experts—such as populous cities flush with diverse industries—these marketplaces could serve to source and coordinate in-person connections. In circumstances with somewhat less obvious local expertise in a given area—particularly in suburban or rural regions or schools where time or transportation is limited—going online and using search features within tools like ImBlaze could enable students to find latent place-based internship opportunities in their own backyard. And in regions where a given industry or expertise is truly absent, online marketplaces could also offer fully *online* connections to mentors and experts beyond the community.

In all such cases, the slots through which students can learn and connect, and the boundaries of school as we know it, could both radically expand.

As a harbinger of that next phase, just as online *learning* tools have started to flip from a VAP to a facilitated network model, so too are innovations in *connecting* making a similar shift (see Figure 5.2). A new set of platforms that can source out-of-school learning experiences or bring outsiders into schools is beginning to crop up.

The market depicted on the right side of this diagram—of innovations in connecting—is far more nascent than the online learning market. As we've already described in chapter 4, a number of tools are emerging in this first phase of disruption, in the form of VAP "connecting" tools. These offer online mentors and experts who can deliver specific college and career advice or offer ongoing support to students through traditional mentorship models. Many such tools include a proprietary product, such as a curriculum or service. Thus, even though they may *enable* new connections

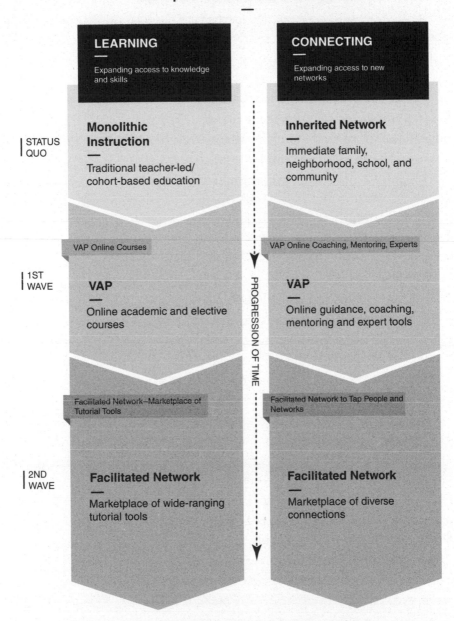

Figure 5.2 Charting Parallel Disruptions in Learning and Connecting

in students' lives, those relationships are a by-product of a VAP business model rather than a facilitated network. These organizations are not serving as brokers. Instead, they are service providers that funnel mentors or coaches into schools, plugging into traditional learning or support structures.

As the market evolves, some tools are shifting away from purely VAP structures toward facilitated network models. For example, schools purchase ImBlaze to add value to their internship programs. By design, however, the platform resembles a facilitated network. It gives schools the ability to build their own proprietary marketplaces of opportunity.

And finally, on the edges of the market, we're beginning to see tools that fit the second wave of disruption, functioning as full-blown facilitated marketplaces. For example, Nepris, the company founded by Sabari Raja to bring experts into classrooms over video chat, brokers connections between experts and teachers looking to bring the real world into classrooms. The tool essentially functions as a two-sided market. Unlike some platforms that pair mentors with specific curricula, Nepris does not sell a curriculum or prescribe what lessons teachers should teach or what experts should offer. Rather, it helps both sides find one another through its platform, and allows teachers to figure out where those online experts might fit into their own lessons or units.

Other marketplace models are set up to broker local, in-person connections. For example, CommunityShare, a small start-up in Tucson, Arizona, is trying to bring big changes to traditional classrooms. According to its founder, educator Josh Schachter, the local, online database functions almost like a Craigslist for teachers who are seeking guest educators and speakers to come into their classrooms. Schachter believes the demand is there: in a survey he conducted of nine thousand teachers from over 250 schools in southern Arizona, 84 percent of respondents said that they wanted more community engagement. The survey also confirmed what Schachter suspected: in the current system, teachers lack time to establish ties to experts in their community and aren't sure where to find them in the first place.[22] CommunityShare steps in as an intermediary that can source and broker these connections between teachers and community members.

Given the early stages of this market, it should hardly come as a surprise that Nepris and CommunityShare have also been approached to white-label their platforms for customers looking to curate and brand their own local or regional expert marketplaces, as ImBlaze does with internships. By customizing these tools to various geographies, Nepris and CommunityShare customers can likewise use the software platforms to populate their own walled gardens with resources and opportunities.

Building a Networking and Opportunity Hub

The emerging schools and tools described in this chapter reflect very early efforts to organize a marketplace of providers that connects students to relationships beyond their school, or to bring the outside world—and the people in it—into schools more deliberately. The particular platforms mentioned here may or may not be the ones that succeed in the long run. Still, they offer a glimpse into the sorts of tools that stand to emerge as the market for out-of-school learning and expanding in-school networks grows.

For such models to thrive, however, schools re-architecting themselves and adopting these tools are only half of the equation. The success of these approaches will hinge on being able to attract a supply of community members near and far who can serve as mentors and experts. Where might this supply of connections come from? To explore how best to tap the latent talent in communities and industries, we will need to better understand what might motivate a wide array of people to engage with schools and students. We tackle that question in chapter 6.

KEY TAKEAWAYS

- The current design of the K–12 education system has few "slots" into which willing experts and mentors can fit. But the disruptive force of online learning is reshaping the architecture of the traditional education system and positioning schools to better embrace additional resources.
- Some emerging school models are using online learning as a backbone to create slots for new learning experiences that incorporate

outside adults into their learning model. Others have long recognized the importance of embracing outsiders. These slots represent critical interfaces where new relationships can be integrated into the education system.

- Over time, innovations in connecting are likely to evolve alongside innovations in learning. For the foreseeable future, we predict that such innovations will be incubated in walled-garden systems that carefully filter outsiders and curate out-of-school learning experiences.

- Eventually, these gardens may become even more permeable, giving way to a facilitated network that can serve as a "marketplace" where students and outside mentors, internship hosts, and the like can find one another. The products offered in this market will enable far more diverse connections than traditional schools can provide.

Notes

1. Christensen, C. M., Johnson, C. W., & Horn, M. B. (2008). *Disrupting class.* New York, NY: McGraw-Hill Professional Publishing.
2. For more on blended learning, see Horn, M. B., & Staker, H. (2014). *Blended: Using disruptive innovation to improve schools.* San Francisco, CA: Jossey-Bass.
3. National Education Association. (2011). Blended learning. Retrieved from http://www.nea.org/assets/docs/PB36blendedlearning2011.pdf
4. Stabell, C. B., & Fjeldstad, Ø. D. (1998). Configuring value for competitive advantage: On chains, shops, and networks. *Strategic Management Journal, 19*(5), 413–437. doi:10.1002/(SICI)1097-0266(199805)19:5<413::AID-SMJ946>3.0.CO;2-C
5. As of 2014, 38 percent of twelfth-graders nationally were proficient in reading (college-ready), and 39 percent of them were proficient in math. These distressing outcomes flow directly from the VAP structures that dominate most schools' approach to instruction. Fields, R. (2014). *Towards the National Assessment of Educational Progress (NAEP) as an indicator of academic preparedness for college and job training.* Washington, DC: National Assessment Governing Board. Retrieved from https://www.nagb.gov/content/nagb/assets/documents/what-we-do/preparedness-research/NAGB-indicator-of-preparedness-report.pdf
6. Here it is useful to note that providers in a facilitated network may themselves offer products and services that fall under VAP models. For example, sellers in an education marketplace could offer tutoring services or prepackaged content.
7. We credit Josh Schachter, founder of the Arizona-based nonprofit CommunityShare, with the phrase "going online to get offline."
8. According to a 2016 case study, Summit students spend sixteen hours per week in "personalized learning time" and demonstrate content mastery by scoring at least

80 percent on assessments taken at the conclusion of each module. Osborne, D. (2016). *Schools of the future: California's Summit Public Schools.* Retrieved from http://www .progressivepolicy.org/wp-content/uploads/2016/01/2016.01-Osborne_Schools-of-the-Future_Californias-Summit-Public-Schools.pdf

9. Ibid.

10. For an example of these listings, see Summit Public Schools. (2015). [MASTER] Student Expedition Course Catalog 2015–16. Retrieved from https://docs.google .com/document/d/1pFyD_FkGhmOQ052maDpNe1ifaUviodX4RxQwkkIHSWA

11. Readers interested in taking a closer look at the Summit approach should see Summit Learning. (2017). The science of Summit: School models that drive student success [Web log post]. Retrieved from https://blog.summitlearning.org/2017/08/science-of-summit-framework-research/

12. Students can earn enough credit to fulfill a single competency in about four weeks and a full credit in about thirty-two to thirty-six weeks. VLACS. (n.d.). Learning through experience. Retrieved from http://vlacs.org/learning-through-experience; VLACS. (n.d.). Flexible learning pathways—Experience. Retrieved from http://vlacs.org/middle-high-school/why-vlacs/why-vlacs-for-students-and-parents/flexible-learning-pathways/learn-through-experience

13. Freeland Fisher, J. (2015, December 14). The next-gen high school to watch [Web log post]. Retrieved from https://www.christenseninstitute.org/blog/the-next-gen-high-school-to-watch

14. Kirsch, Z. (2017, May 23). The new diploma mills. *Slate.* Retrieved from http://www .slate.com/articles/news_and_politics/schooled/2017/05/u_s_high_schools_may_be_over_relying_on_online_credit_recovery_to_boost.html

15. Using small-group and one-on-one instruction as a base, teachers can begin to better customize each student's individual educational experience by pulling from a wide array of force multipliers, including online learning, experiences, expeditions, and internships. Looking ahead, in models that leverage both online learning and out-of-school experts, the role of the teacher will shift in some important ways. But it's worth noting that there is little evidence to suggest that computers will replace teachers. In a far more likely scenario, teachers stand to become more like "learner advocates," carefully weaving a wide array of educational experiences—traditional classes, tutoring, cocurricular experiences, and team-based projects alike—into a coherent educational path for their students. We credit Amy Anderson and Rebecca Kisner of ReSchool Colorado for the term *learner advocate,* which ReSchool uses in its work to connect students with a broad range of learning opportunities and experiences. For further reading on the field's ongoing discussion about whether computers will replace teachers, see the following: Arnett, T. (2016). Teaching in the machine age: How innovation can make bad teachers good and good teachers better. Retrieved from https://www.christenseninstitute.org/publications/teaching-machine-age

16. Osborne, *Schools of the future.*

17. Berdick, C. (2016, August 4). Inside the online school that could radically change how kids learn everywhere. *Wired.* Retrieved from https://www.wired.com/2016/08/inside-online-school-radically-change-kids-learn-everywhere

18. Dustin, E. (2017, April 12). From the field: How virtual, personalized learning built VLACS [Web log post]. Retrieved from https://motivislearning.com/insights/from-the-field-interview-steve-kossakoski-vlacs

19. Big Picture Learning. (n.d.). 10 distinguishers. Retrieved from http://www.bigpicture .org/apps/pages/index.jsp?uREC_ID=389353&type=d&pREC_ID=902235; Big Picture

Learning. (n.d.). How it works. Retrieved from http://www.bigpicture.org/apps/pages/index.jsp?uREC_ID=389353&type=d&pREC_ID=882356

20. Arnold, K. D., Wartman, K. L., Brown, P. G., Gismondi, A. N., Pesce, J. R., & Stanfield, D. (2016). The connector study: A strategy for collecting post-graduation data about low-income high school students. *Journal of Education for Students Placed at Risk (JESPAR), 21*(3), 174–189. doi:10.1080/10824669.2016.1172230

21. Christensen, C., & Raynor, M. (2013). *The innovator's solution: Creating and sustaining successful growth.* Boston, MA: Harvard Business Review Press.

22. CommunityShare. (n.d.). Why share? Retrieved from http://www.communityshare.us/why-share

CHAPTER SIX

If You Build It, Will They Connect?

Engaging Outsiders inside Schools

"Boom, Boom, Boom!"

Leave it to YouTube to preserve cringe-worthy videos for posterity. In one of them, you can find serial entrepreneur Jeff Taylor yelling *"Boom, boom, boom!"* into the camera, smiling widely and triumphantly, thrusting his fists in the air.

In 2006, Taylor was fresh off his wildly successful stint as CEO of Monster.com, an online jobs database, which he founded in 1994 and rapidly built into a multimillion-dollar business. The video was a commercial for Taylor's latest internet venture, Eons.com, a social network for Americans over the age of fifty. "Boom, boom, boom" was a not-so-subtle nod to the site's target audience: baby boomers. Boomers were an especially hot demographic at the time: there were seventy-eight million of them, and they spent more than $2 trillion annually. Companies like Eons were rushing to capitalize on the generation's transition from corporate life into retirement.[1]

With the rise of social networking all around, a social networking site for older Americans seemed like a tempting venture. In addition to their extraordinary spending power, an estimated forty-four million older people were already online.

Taylor believed there was an opportunity to build an online community that flipped the typical experience of growing older on its head. In addition to providing the opportunity to connect with people their same age, Eons.com offered boomers "games, brain-builders, and movie reviews," pointers on how to manage savings, and even cRANKy—a customized "age-relevant" search engine that would yield only the top four search results relevant to older people.[2]

"Let's live to be one hundred, or die trying!" Taylor yelled into the camera. "Be proud, be inspired, get it done, and you know what's coming . . . *boom, boom, boom!*"

Leveraging his success at Monster.com, Taylor raised $32 million from leading venture capital firms.[3] But by 2008, despite much hype and advertising, the site was drawing just shy of three hundred thousand unique visitors a month—less than 1 percent of the originally identified market.[4] Not long after the website's launch, Taylor laid off 40 percent of his staff. Eons sputtered along, but in 2011, Taylor sold the site for an undisclosed amount.[5] One year later, Eons quietly closed its doors.

Some might guess that older adults simply had no interest in social media. But by 2016, boomers were migrating online in droves: 72 percent of Americans between the ages of fifty and sixty-four and 62 percent of Americans over sixty-five were using Facebook.[6]

Getting at the Job to Be Done

In the end, Eons.com could have taken a page from Thoreau. Watching the rush to technological progress in the nineteenth century, the famously reclusive writer observed, "We are in great haste to construct a magnetic telegraph from Maine to Texas; but Maine and Texas, it may be, have nothing important to communicate." More bluntly: just because two people are old doesn't make them old friends.

Schools and tools aiming to expand students' access to networks through online, networked platforms should take note.

Technology today can connect people at the press of a button. If we hope to expand students' networks, the challenge facing schools is not creating the perfect technology to connect people. Technically speaking, advances over the past decade in communications technologies have brought this entirely within reach. Instead, the biggest lift will be creating networked tools and experiences that *motivate people from diverse backgrounds to connect in new ways.*

Taylor's experience suggests that urging people to forge new social connections is not always an easy task. As chapter 5 described, we anticipate a marked increase in facilitated networks for schools—be those walled gardens or open marketplaces—where students can forge new and stronger connections. For these marketplaces to successfully scale, however, outside adults will need to be willing to engage in our school systems at unprecedented rates.

As tempting as it may be, a "build it and they will come" approach like Taylor's won't suffice. Instead of just building new platforms, we need to understand the *circumstances* that drive people to invest in relationships, particularly new relationships that stretch beyond their existing, inherited networks. From there, networking tools can emerge to start to expand students' networks in exciting new ways.

One of the flaws in Taylor's approach to Eons.com was starting where many entrepreneurs often begin: a market defined by demographics. Taylor built Eons specifically to help the baby boomer generation—and to exclude everyone outside of that group. Demographics are the easiest way for organizations to think about the contours of their customer or user base. Today, with the explosion of data availability, companies are better than ever at knowing who buys what products. Many even gather demographic details of every person who clicks on their digital advertisements.

Segmenting a market by traditional demographics like age, race, or gender may reveal *correlations* in consumer behaviors. But it is rarely useful in arriving at *causation*. A person's demographics don't ever *cause* her to do something. Instead, from the customer's or user's perspective, the world is filled with problems that she would like to solve in an attempt to make progress in her life.

In the language of innovation theory, we can think of the progress we all want to make in life as a "job." We go out and "hire" a product or service to perform that job. And in industry after industry, we've seen that an understanding of users' *jobs to be done* is the key to getting market segmentation and product design right.[7]

Jobs include functional, emotional, and even social components. Unpacking these components may help explain why boomers hired Facebook instead of Eons.com. Rather than banishing them to Baby

Boomer Island, Facebook performs for older people many of the jobs that it does for everyone else: functionally, it helps them fill downtime in their day and communicate with their social networks online. Socially, it makes them feel integrated into their community and family, and cared for by far-flung friendships of their past. Emotionally, it helps them feel connected to younger generations and entertained—and maybe, in the end, even a little bit younger.[8]

A Milkshake Is More Than a Milkshake

To understand how jobs shape all sorts of customer behaviors, consider a product as seemingly simple as a milkshake.[9] Many years ago, Clay Christensen's colleague served as a consultant for a fast-food restaurant chain determined to turn around stagnant milkshake sales. Focus groups of carefully selected customers had offered all kinds of feedback related to creating the perfect milkshake; but even with marked improvements to the product's flavor and texture, milkshake sales simply would not budge.

To try to unearth new insights, the researcher began spending hours outside the restaurant. He observed which customers were buying milkshakes and when. The next day, he returned and began asking anyone he saw walking out with a milkshake, "What job did you *hire* this milkshake to do in your life?" The results were revealing: in the morning, many lone customers admitted that they had long commutes ahead of them. They were "hiring" the milkshake to fight boredom and malaise during their daily drive. Although they did not yet feel hungry, they knew that if they didn't eat anything, they'd feel famished and unproductive by 10 a.m. They were rushing to work, could not afford to spill anything on their clothes, and only had a single free hand.

The researcher realized that for these milkshake enthusiasts, the drink consistently *outcompeted* the other options these commuters contemplated each morning: bagels were too dry, and spreading the cream cheese was annoying and dangerous while they were driving. Candy bars, meanwhile, produced feelings of guilt, and the healthier option of bananas just wasn't filling enough. The milkshake, in contrast to these other products, did an excellent job of filling commuters' time and bellies. It took about twenty minutes to consume, occupied much of the commute, and filled the customers up until lunchtime.

The consultant also witnessed another spike in milkshake consumption in the afternoon. These customers tended to be parents with young children coming in for lunch. They were purchasing the milkshakes for their kids. When pressed to explain why they had "hired" the milkshakes, they admitted to the consultant that they were simply tired of having to say no. Milkshakes, in other words, helped them feel like loving (or, at least, less guilty) parents.

It turned out, then, that there were at least two very different jobs that the milkshakes were performing at two different times of the day. Suffice it to say, next time you buy a milkshake, you're probably looking to achieve a larger purpose than just getting a sugar high.

Understanding a job is not just about identifying a need in someone's life. Rather, it requires an understanding of the *circumstances* that arise in people's lives prompting them to hire particular solutions. Understanding those circumstances is arguably as important as understanding people themselves.

Jobs-to-be-done theory helps companies better understand the actual business they're in. As it turned out, the fast-food chain wasn't really selling milkshakes at all. Rather, it was selling relief from boring commutes and energy slumps in the morning, and selling some small assurance that parents felt more devoted to their children in the afternoon. The theory also revealed the size and contours of the market, and the true identity of competitors: milkshakes weren't only competing against other fast-food milkshakes (an assumption that focus groups often begin with, which in turn often leads product designers into an arms race to add more and more features). Instead, the plane of competition was more complex and varied. Milkshakes were contending against bagels, bananas, and parents' bargaining chip with their kids other than sweets—video games.

With these insights, the fast-food chain could start thinking about ways to sell more milkshakes to match these *circumstances*—rather than trying to create the platonic ideal of a milkshake based on focus-group feedback. To tackle the morning commute job, for example, it could thicken the shakes to make them last longer, or add small chunks of fruit to surprise customers and help combat boredom. To tackle the afternoon job, the chain could add toys to keep children busy for an extra few minutes as their guilt-ridden parents looked on.[10]

In a nutshell, jobs-to-be-done theory is a tool to better understand customer motivation and engagement. Schools and innovators looking to increase students' social capital can take a page from the parable of the milkshake: if we can understand the jobs of prospective mentors, students, and teachers we can in turn build tools and experiences that they'll be excited to hire.

Mentors' Various Jobs to Be Done

If a new, networked school system is going to manage bringing a whole host of relationships to bear, it can learn a thing or two from an industry that has spent decades trying to do just that: the mentoring world. Historically, youth mentorship programs have faced a litany of challenges trying to attract prospective mentors, convert them into actual participants, and then retain the best among them. Each stage of the process presents its own set of hurdles.

Mentorship programs consistently grapple with the chasm between adults' stated interest in mentorship and those who actually step up: although more than nine out of ten of Americans express a *desire* to volunteer, only 25 percent end up actually doing so.[11] Research into this disconnect has revealed various factors—time constraints, lack of interest in positions that may not sufficiently leverage their expertise, and sometimes even feelings of inadequacy—that people claim stand in the way of stepping up to lend their services.[12]

Yet to build a system that increases students' social capital, schools and communities will need to start to cross this chasm and successfully recruit and retain more and more willing adults into the school system. The answer is probably not just to ask more often or more loudly for people to help. Instead, schools and mentoring organizations should begin to use jobs-to-be-done analysis to cut through some of the limitations and noise in the volunteer space.

We do not pretend to have a comprehensive understanding of all of these jobs, but we do believe that we can make some educated guesses.[13]

From a formal or informal mentor's perspective, connecting with a young person may perform one or more of a variety of jobs in his life:

1. Help me feel connected or less lonely.
2. Help me feel younger or connected to the young and keep my brain sharp.
3. Help me show my friends that I'm socially responsible.
4. Help me feel less guilty about being a "lucky" person.
5. Help me feel useful and put me to work.
6. Help me feel that I'm "paying it forward" to someone like me.
7. Help me feel like an expert by sharing my skills with another person.

As we mentioned, these are our best guesses at some of the jobs that could prompt an adult to hire mentorship in his life. To unearth the actual jobs, mentoring organizations will need to conduct jobs-based interviews to understand why the people in their community are (or aren't) hiring mentoring programs as solutions in their lives.[14] From there, they will be able to successfully innovate by integrating around a particular job or set of jobs identified in the course of their research.

To understand how this might work in practical terms, consider what the host of unlikely "competitors" might be if we think a prospective mentor is looking for solutions that "Help me show my friends that I'm socially responsible." To satisfy this job, an individual could hire recycling bins that make visible her commitment to environmental responsibility; she could buy more books about prevailing social issues and prominently display them on her bookshelf for guests to see. *Or* she could sign up as a mentor at the local elementary school to help a third-grader learn to read. In other words, as crass as it may sound, mentors may not be seeking out mentoring opportunities because they "want to mentor." Rather, they are probably trying to get something done in their lives, and have decided that mentorship is the best means to that end.

By this logic, mentoring organizations are not just competing against other volunteer efforts to recruit mentors. They compete against a wide range of solutions that someone could conceivably hire to perform a particular job—such as combating loneliness or paying it forward.

Once a mentoring organization or school understands the true plane of competition for volunteers' time, it can better brand and design its model around the various jobs that mentors are hiring mentorship to perform. If some mentors, for example, are looking to satisfy the job of "help me show my friends I'm socially responsible," an organization could integrate features that help mentors show their friends that they're involved in their communities. It could inaugurate a "mentor of the month" plaque that mentors could display in their homes, post pictures of an associated awards ceremony on Facebook, or simply provide opportunities for mentors to easily share their efforts through their own social media pages.[15]

The possibilities of such design decisions will depend on a clearer understanding of the particular jobs driving people to hire mentorship in a given community. However, once they understand what people are actually trying to get done in their lives, organizations stand to attract and retain mentors far more seamlessly than they have in the past.

Jobs Transcend Demographic Categories

Mentorship programs, of course, are just one of many examples of a field looking to engage people in networked models that reach young people. With this kind of mindset, *any* organization looking to broker connections between adults and students—be it a formal mentoring program, a tutoring company, an edtech tool, or even a school itself—could begin to break down barriers and bring more and varied relationships into students' lives.

Consider the example of CNA Speaking Exchange, the video-based language technology that connects Brazilian students with volunteers from US-based retirement homes (discussed in chapter 4). The model is premised on a potentially large supply of English-speaking senior-citizen volunteers, a sizable demographic in the US. But CNA has actually found that it's quite difficult to scale beyond the handful of senior centers from which it currently draws volunteers. Senior living facilities can be difficult to work with. If there isn't an employee on-site willing to set up the technology and organize sessions, the online connections end up unreliable at best.[16]

But in searching for English-speaking conversation partners, CNA could instead consider the market through the lens of jobs to be done. The jobs that seniors likely hire CNA to perform—for example, "Help me feel more connected and less lonely," "Help me fill up my quiet morning," and "Help me keep my brain sharp"—are not necessarily limited to senior home retirees resisting isolation and aging. In fact, many people of varying ages are likely to share those jobs. CNA could, for example, extend their marketing efforts to target divorcees, "empty nest" parents whose children have just left for college, or even millennials living alone for the first time.

Other edtech innovations have done just that: expressly embraced movement *away* from the constraints of marketing to, or recruiting along, traditional demographic dimensions. Granny Cloud, for example, is now replete with volunteers who are not actually "grannies." The organization quickly realized that the granny role—sweetly encouraging and motivating students in the developing world—is merely symbolic of the broader circumstance of someone hoping to be kind and help children. As it turns out, interest in volunteering on Granny Cloud far exceeds its initial demographic. Now grannies consist of males and females as young as twenty-four and as old as seventy-eight.[17]

This is not to say that organizations have to dismiss demographics entirely; after understanding the underlying jobs to be done, program designers and recruiters can layer demographic data *on top of* those jobs to reveal *personas*—that is, profiles of people who are trying to get a particular job done and have particular demographic attributes, such as gender or age. This can help recruiting and marketing efforts to target customers even more effectively. All too often, however, companies fixate on personas *before* analyzing the underlying jobs that drive consumption or adoption. This approach would have constrained Granny Cloud to solely recruiting among literal older ladies—a far narrower population of volunteers than the organization has found to be viable in the long run.

"Unbundling" across Jobs

Jobs-to-be-done theory can help unearth the drivers that could bring more people into schools. But it's also worth noting that today *mentorship* is a general term that often describes a wide variety of roles and relationships in students' lives. In addition to formal mentors of the Big Brothers, Big Sisters variety, young people also have informal mentors, such as sports coaches, neighbors, and even older children. As technology solutions begin to scale, these more informal relationships are beginning to include brief digital encounters—what some have dubbed "flash mentoring"—with adults, facilitated by innovations like Nepris and iCouldBe.

People participating in these relationships are hiring mentorship for a variety of reasons. Applying the milkshake analogy, some are the proverbial hungry commuters, and others the metaphorical guilty parents. Still others choose not to hire mentoring. In order to maximize adult participation in the project of expanding students' social capital, mentorship organizations might be best served to target a few of these jobs very well—rather than trying to be everything to everyone.

Other industries demonstrate how such "unbundling" across jobs can unfold. Take newspapers, for example. Before the dawn of the internet, in their previous (and more prosperous) lives newspapers operated across a variety of consumer demands, performing a range of entirely separate jobs. Among many functions, newspapers helped readers[18]

1. Find employment through classified ads.
2. Locate bargains on low-cost products to purchase in their free time.
3. Find an opinion columnist or contributor with similar views and/or who could clarify their beliefs.
4. Stay informed about recent events in their community or the world.

These are just a few of the many jobs readers hired newspapers to do. The newspaper industry, however, has begun to unravel: customers are hiring other products that perform one of these *discrete* jobs far better than traditional newspapers ever could. Customers can scour Amazon and Cars .com for low-cost products small and large, and have those items on their doorstep by the next day. They can hop onto partisan news websites like *Breitbart* or *Slate* or they can scroll through their friends' Facebook feed to find opinion writers who will confirm their beliefs.[19] And Craigslist has taken online classified ads for everything from furniture sales to apartment rentals.

Meanwhile, readers now turn to online outlets to find the most up-to-date news, and can even use tools that aggregate sources, such as Google

Alerts, to obtain real-time, highly relevant news on specific topics. And finally, in a twist of innovation irony, a handful of websites, initially led by Jeff Taylor's Monster.com, that connect prospective employees with prospective employers have made newspapers' job listings seem like relics from the Stone Age.[20]

Newspapers and mentorship may have a fair amount in common. As a term and concept, "mentoring" encompasses a wide range of activities and types of relationships. Moreover, perhaps because they are so focused on recruiting, mentorship programs and schools aiming to attract additional adults into students' lives risk trying to be everything to everyone, much as newspapers did in their heyday.

But to successfully scale and thrive, mentorship efforts may have to unbundle their efforts around the various jobs that their mentors hire them to perform in their lives—with an understanding that these experiences may look different from each other.

It's worth noting that some extent of unbundling is occurring in mentorship programs that leverage "many-to-many" mentoring models—meaning that they provide group mentoring opportunities or offer multiple mentors at a time to high-need students. These efforts are often billed as mitigating the time constraints associated with traditional one-on-one relationships. This is seemingly rational given the variables that we know matter: these models recognize that students often benefit from a "web" of relationships with multiple adults, and likewise are designed to alleviate the time burden that many adults cite as a barrier to becoming mentors in the first place.[21]

As logical as team or group mentoring may be, it runs the risk of getting the categories that drive program design wrong. This team model treats *time*—rather than circumstances—as the unit that needs to be unbundled. Simply dividing the time commitment required of mentors may do little to satisfy their various jobs to be done. In fact, if someone becomes a mentor in an effort to feel less lonely, curtailing her time commitment could *demotivate* rather than bolster her involvement in a given program.[22]

All of this may sound like a lot of work for schools, mentoring nonprofits, or bootstrapped edtech start-ups with limited resources. But the key to remember is that organizing around jobs substantially *opens up* the size of a market. Rather than jockeying for a share of the 25 percent of people who currently end up volunteering, mentoring organizations could begin to understand how to draw in more of the 65 percent of people who express a *willingness* to volunteer but choose not to. And that figure just in the US quite literally encompasses more than one hundred million prospective mentors. Imagine being able to tap into that incredible fount of capacity and support in more young people's lives.

What Are Students Hiring For?

Ensuring that more adults are willing to engage with students and schools is only half the battle. If a facilitated network of new relationships is going to take root, students and their teachers must themselves start to hire more and diverse relationships into their lives.

It may feel odd to classify students as customers, but doing so provides powerful insight into why many of them struggle to stay motivated in school. As our colleagues at the Clayton Christensen Institute have written about in the past, motivation research suggests at least two jobs to be done in students' lives: they want to feel successful, and they want to have fun with their friends.[23]

Students could hire school to perform these jobs in their lives, but they don't *have to.* Metaphorical bagels and bananas that compete with school abound. To feel successful, students could just as easily join a sports team or play video games (many of which specialize in instant gratification) instead. To have fun with friends, they could hire the math class that some of their friends attend. But they could likewise talk to friends on social media or goof off in class.

Put differently, jobs-to-be-done theory can reveal an entirely new perspective on what the education system often categorizes as "unmotivated" or "disengaged" students. Such students are not choosing in a vacuum to work less hard or drop out. In fact, those decisions are themselves *hiring* decisions: unmotivated students *fire* school because they *hire* other alternatives that better align around what they are trying to get done.[24]

Unfortunately, by its very design, our education system often inadvertently encourages them to do so. Students want to feel successful, but may

find that they can only achieve that feeling by participating in extracurricular activities that naturally filter them into areas in which they are
more likely to excel. If a student is tall for her age, she can join the
basketball or volleyball team—and experience a reasonably high probability
of success. If a student is naturally inclined toward public speaking or
performing arts, he can join the drama club, again with the reasonable
expectation of success.[25]

Schools, however, have struggled to bring these same principles to bear
in academics. In most schools, students take a test every few weeks, then
wait another couple of weeks to receive their results, hardly arming them
with even small successes. Time to have fun with friends over lunch or
recess is often wholly separate from time to "learn." The classroom all too
often depends on students sitting quietly in rows and being asked to
ignore—rather than engage with—their friends. As a result, students may
find themselves less and less inclined to hire school to get their most
pressing jobs done.

This disconnect reveals just how often schools can fall into the trap of
designing for what students "need" rather than what they actually demand.

Jobs, it should be noted, are not synonymous with needs. For example,
a subset of the commuters hiring milkshakes may have *needed* a healthier
breakfast to keep their weight in check. But the sugary drink that they *hired*
reflected the job they were trying to get done and the fact that milkshakes
were best engineered to satisfy that job. In school, we may presume that
students *need* to learn literacy, numeracy, and critical thinking—but
students themselves may not be demanding those things. As a result,
schools must think about how to best design the learning environment to
increase the likelihood that students enthusiastically hire—and engage in—
school.

The good news is that schools can leverage this understanding of
students' jobs to be done to redesign themselves to engage more students
in *learning and connecting*. For example, innovative school models like
Summit and VLACS, discussed in chapter 5, are designed to give students
more frequent, formative feedback and to provide social learning experiences with teams and projects. And Big Picture Learning takes a page from
the ways in which extracurriculars have always excelled—enabling students
to peg their learning against their natural interests or inclinations, whereby

they may be more likely to feel successful according to their own definitions of success.

Innovations offering students new connections will also benefit from carefully architecting themselves around students' jobs to be done. For example, Student Success Agency offers near-peer mentors who are closer to students' age; this likely increases students' ability to see their collegeage agents as more like friends than as older, authoritative guidance counselors. At the same time, these college students can make success more concrete: agents help high schoolers see people like them who have had success in making it through the college application process and into college.

Other models are likewise architected to ensure that students experience shorter-term "wins" even between tests. For example, using the online tutoring software, if students run into a problem that they can't solve, tutors can immediately address those challenges and help students successfully solve problems—rather than having to wait days or even weeks for their teachers to address misunderstanding.

That said, all sorts of designs could pander to consumer motivation while not actually improving people's lives. Understanding stakeholder jobs may be different than determining goals. In the education system, this distinction is crucial. If schools were to focus only on designing for students' jobs to be done, they might abandon other important goals. For example, were schools to simply convert themselves into daylong recess hubs, students might gleefully have fun with friends all day without learning a single thing.

The same could occur in efforts to build systems that help students connect. In her sweeping account of teens' online social behaviors, danah boyd, Microsoft research scientist and founder of the Data & Society Research Institute, provides a troubling example of how this might play out.[26] In her book *It's Complicated*, boyd describes how during the 2006–2007 school year, competition between MySpace and Facebook began to heat up. "The presence of two competing services would not be particularly interesting if it weren't for the makeup of the participants on each site. During that school year, as teens chose between MySpace and Facebook, race and class were salient factors in describing which teens used which service," she wrote. "The driving force was obvious: teens focused their attention on the site where their friends were socializing. In doing so, their choices reified the race and class divisions that existed within their schools."[27]

In other words, students' job to be done—have fun with friends—was clearly motivating which platform they hired. As a result, it was widening divides among different groups of students. Their preferences were rooted in deep-seated beliefs about the cultural differences between Facebook and MySpace.[28]

boyd's findings are a stark reminder that jobs-to-be-done framing only reveals the motivations behind consumer behavior; it will not always lead to better "outcomes" such as expanding opportunity or diversifying networks as we've discussed in the book thus far. In other words, young people may be flocking to online networks in droves, but their hiring these networks may not be translating into new or better opportunities.

This suggests that pursuing innovations that broaden, deepen, and diversify student networks will require *deliberate designs* that accomplish two things at once. First, innovative platforms and school models must cater to the jobs of students, mentors, and teachers—so that they will happily hire a relationship or a tool or platform that helps them connect. Second, these new models must then create experiences that not only cater to their jobs but also leverage designs that accomplish systemic goals such as engagement, academic success, or expanded networks of opportunity.

By targeting these goals, schools can also begin to meet different stakeholders' jobs as well: teachers.

Why Teachers Hire Schools and Tools

If we hope to broker new and deeper connections between schools and the real world, teachers have a crucial role to play. Given that many facilitated networks will for the foreseeable future function as walled gardens, teachers will represent a key gating mechanism that can either hinder or radically expand students' access to networks, depending on the tools they are willing to hire. Therefore, innovators seeking to better connect students to mentors must stay attuned to what teachers are demanding.

Why might a teacher hire a tool like Nepris or iCouldBe or ImBlaze? And how could teachers themselves architect interactions between students and mentors or experts to help both students and outside adults best satisfy their jobs to be done?

To tackle this, we need to understand first and foremost why teachers have hired teaching in their lives. Although this is an enormous research question unto itself, surveys suggest that many teachers go into their profession because they believe they will be good at it, and seek achievement and recognition that affirms this belief. Many are also motivated by the nature of the work itself, and hire teaching to feel that they are making a difference in the lives of their students.[29]

Barriers to progress along these dimensions abound, however.

Despite the best efforts of teachers, the design of the system often makes these core motivations difficult to satisfy. Teachers are expected to support high numbers of students at once—making it challenging to muster a sense that they are producing meaningful progress among their many individual students. Teachers also often take on significant administrative tasks that draw them away from the students they signed up to teach in the first place. Moreover, a litany of large-scale factors operating beyond school—such as entrenched poverty and institutionalized racism—erect obstacles to student learning that even the best educators may struggle to overcome.

Such circumstances prevent many teachers from consistently experiencing a sense of achievement or from feeling as though they are making a difference in their school communities and in the lives of their students.

But barriers to progress frequently present opportunities for innovation. Tools that connect students with additional mentors and supports could play an especially important role. For teachers struggling to engage students with a wide range of interests, innovations like Nepris can help teachers show their students that learning can be fun, interesting, and relevant—in turn easing the teaching and learning process inside the classroom. Online tutoring and supports can temporarily distribute classroom management responsibilities to other, online adults, opening up critical room to help teachers feel as though they're doing the most for their students in the limited amount of time they have. These are just a few examples of how tools could be designed to satisfy teachers' jobs to be done.[30]

Using Jobs to Reach Your Goals

In attempting to construct a well-oiled machine that nurtures and expands networks, schools and mentoring organizations could fall into the trap of construing the fixed *goals* of a school or tool with users' *jobs*. This would be a mistake: the concepts are not synonymous, even though they can work in concert.

For a company like a fast-food restaurant or a website, jobs-to-be-done theory simply reveals that making money can come about from a deeper understanding of the business that you're actually in—such as keeping commuters happy or easing parents' guilt. For many organizations, the ultimate goal at hand is relatively blunt: get people to buy stuff. Fast-food chains successfully integrating around the jobs of hungry commuters or tired parents do so in an effort to increase their bottom line.

But for educators, mentoring organizations, and students, meeting their jobs to be done has different implications. Instead of driving profit, creating solutions that can satisfy adults' and students' jobs can yield even more valuable nonmonetary returns: accomplishing often hard-to-reach targets of student engagement, teacher or volunteer retention, and parent satisfaction.

Bearing this in mind, to innovate successfully, education systems looking to expand students' networks must avoid the constant temptation to design solutions around narrowly construed goals, such as getting young people into college. Somewhat counterintuitively, building the perfect intervention or curriculum to achieve those goals may miss the mark. A mentor does not hire a volunteer opportunity to get a student one transactional step closer to college. He has his own job in mind. Similarly, young people looking to further their life prospects do not hire mentoring to successfully fill out a FAFSA form. That needs to get done, but it is not a job to be done. Rather, students likely want to feel successful or simply to feel seen or heard. Solutions need to cater to those deeper motivations.

Defining the Metrics of Success

That said, nailing a job can still function as a *means* rather than an end. Student motivation and engagement offer incredible hooks to reach higher-order, often challenging goals facing schools. For example, a 2015 Gallup poll found that only 50 percent of students are "engaged in school" and that fewer than half are "hopeful." The same poll found that students who are both engaged and hopeful are nearly five times more likely to report that they "do well in school" compared to their disengaged or unhopeful counterparts.[31] In other words, increasing engagement can leverage better outcomes against metrics that the system at large is aiming to achieve.

And all this, of course, will depend on how we measure success in a networked school system. How we construe the goals of the education system will shape the innovations we pursue. What gets measured generally gets done. If the metrics that we employ to assess the success of the education system—blunt instruments like test scores and college matriculation rates—remain constant, we could easily architect a system that gets better and better at the wrong thing, by the wrong criteria.

If schools simply cram new relationship-expanding tools and models into the current system, innovations that have the potential to expand students' access to social capital will be relegated to hollow, one-off transactions, rather than authentic opportunities to foster relationships.

In short, measurement matters. And incorporating social capital measures will be a challenging but critical task for this next wave of school innovation. As one researcher famously put it, social capital is "fiendishly difficult to measure; not because of a recognized paucity of data, but because we do not quite know what we should be measuring."[32] In chapter 7, we will consider policy frameworks and metrics that could ensure deeper investment into expanding students' social capital, and the protections and quality-control measures that will need to be in place along the way.

KEY TAKEAWAYS

- Most companies organize markets by product category and customer demographic—often missing the real motivations behind consumer behavior.
- From the customer's perspective, the world is vastly more complex; customers want to make some sort of progress in their lives. We can

think of this progress as a "job" that customers might "hire" a product or service to perform.

- Successful innovations tend to be tightly integrated around a customer job. Innovations designed to increase students' social capital are no exception. New tools and school designs will need to take the jobs of all stakeholders—mentors, students, and teachers—into account.

- Designing solutions that can satisfy adults' and students' jobs can yield critical nonmonetary returns: nailing often hard-to-reach targets of student engagement, teacher or volunteer retention, and parent satisfaction.

Notes

1. Greene, K. (2006, July 25). Still sexy at 60? *Wall Street Journal*. Retrieved from https://www.wsj.com/articles/SB115379490208516195
2. Sturtevant, R. (2006, November 2). eons.com TV commercial (120 seconds) [Video file]. Retrieved from https://www.youtube.com/watch?v=HhA97pJ8lcg
3. Chen, C. (2008, May 5). Monster.com founder's new venture to die for. *NBC News*. Retrieved from http://www.nbcnews.com/id/24394324/ns/technology_and_science-internet/t/monstercom-founders-new-venture-die
4. Our market penetration calculation divides the total number of unique visitors to Eons.com each month, as of February 2008, by the total number of baby boomer internet users originally identified by Taylor (forty-four million). If we were to account for the growth in the number of older internet users between 2006 and 2008, the ratio would likely be even lower. Schonfeld, E. (2008, February 13). Boomer social network Eons gets a facelift; Spins off obits section as tributes. *TechCrunch*. Retrieved from https://techcrunch.com/2008/02/13/boomer-social-network-eons-gets-a-facelift-spins-off-obits-section-as-tributes
5. Connolly, J. (2001, April 29). Jeff Taylor's $32M baby, Eons.com, sold for undisclosed terms. *Boston Business Journal*. Retrieved from http://www.bizjournals.com/boston/news/2011/04/29/eonscom-sold-for-undisclosed-terms.html
6. Greenwood, S., Perrin, A., & Duggan, M. (2016). Social media update 2016. *Pew Research Center, 11*. Retrieved from http://www.pewinternet.org/2016/11/11/social-media-update-2016
7. The following commentary draws heavily from decades of research on jobs theory summarized in the *Harvard Business Review* article "The 'Jobs to Be Done' Theory of Innovation" and the book *Competing against Luck*. Green Carmichael, S. (2016, December 8). The "jobs to be done" theory of innovation. *Harvard Business Review*. Retrieved from https://hbr.org/ideacast/2016/12/the-jobs-to-be-done-theory-of-innovation; Christensen, C. M., Dillon, K., Hall, T., & Duncan, D. S. (2016).

Competing against luck: The story of innovation and customer choice. New York, NY: HarperBusiness.

8. Pirc, J. (2012, January 12). Parental discretion advised [Web log post]. Retrieved from http://blog.lab42.com/parental-discretion-advised; Rogers, K. (2016, April 14). Why do older people love Facebook? Let's ask my dad. *New York Times.* Retrieved from https://www.nytimes.com/2016/04/15/technology/why-do-older-people-love-facebook-lets-ask-my-dad.html

9. In other words, the theory explains the business you're in, the size and shape of the market, and who the competitors are. For additional examples see Christensen et al., *Competing against luck,* pp. 67–73.

10. Ibid.

11. Yotopoulos, A. (2016, November 3). Three reasons why people don't volunteer, and what can be done about it [Web log post]. Retrieved from http://longevity.stanford.edu/blog/2016/11/03/three-reasons-why-people-dont-volunteer-and-what-can-be-done-about-it

12. Feelings of inadequacy may reflect either an assessment on the part of the prospective volunteer that she is unqualified or an idealized notion of volunteerism. For example, Claremont Graduate University psychology professor Allen Omoto noted, "Sometimes people look at volunteers and see them as being somehow more noble or moral than they themselves are." Davis, M. H. (2005). Becoming (and remaining) a community volunteer: Does personality matter? In A. M. Omoto (ed.), *The Claremont symposium on applied social psychology: Processes of community change and social action* (pp. 67–82). Mahwah, NJ: Lawrence Erlbaum; Clary, E. G., Snyder, M., Ridge, R. D., Copeland, J., Stukas, A. A., Haugen, J., & Miene, P. (1998). Understanding and assessing the motivations of volunteers: A functional approach. *Journal of Personality and Social Psychology, 74*(6), 1516–1530. doi:10.1037/0022-3514.74.6.1516; Beck, E. (2015, December 9). Why don't people volunteer? *PTO Today.* Retrieved from https://www.ptotoday.com/pto-today-articles/article/5940-why-dont-people-volunteer

13. There has been no previous attempt that we are aware of to identify the jobs to be done of mentors. This is our take on what some of these jobs could be, based on what we can meaningfully derive from the body of research on volunteerism and philanthropy, and on the many discussions we (particularly Julia) have had over the years with mentoring organizations and other entities seeking to expand students' access to social capital. We recognize that this list may be incomplete, and welcome further research on this topic. Jobs to be done can be highly specific, and frequently have complex socioemotional dimensions. Individual mentoring organizations should develop theories around what job or set of jobs they are performing.

14. One good guide to these interviews is contained in Spiek, C., & Moesta, B. (2014). *The Jobs-to-be-Done handbook: Practical techniques for improving your application of Jobs-to-be-Done.* CreateSpace Independent Publishing Platform.

15. Our intent is not to propose these social media examples as prescriptive solutions. Rather, we use them here to help explain how mentoring organizations can begin to think about integrating around the jobs of mentors.

16. Author interview with Luciana Locks, March 13, 2017.

17. School in the Cloud. (n.d.). The granny cloud. Retrieved from https://www.theschoolinthecloud.org/people/the-granny-cloud

18. Christensen et al., *Competing against luck.*

19. Although both *Breitbart* and *Slate* may not directly advertise themselves as partisan sources, an analysis from the Pew Research Center showed that, among popular news

sources, *Politico* and *Slate* have the most "consistently liberal" audience, whereas *Breitbart* had one of the most "consistently conservative" audiences, closely ranked with sources such as the *Drudge Report*. Mitchell, A., Gottfried, J., Kiley, J., & Matsa, K.E. (2014). Political polarization & media habits. *Pew Research Center, 21*. Retrieved from http://www.journalism.org/2014/10/21/political-polarization-media-habits

20. For more on newspaper unbundling and how some outlets have fought back, see Christensen et al., *Competing against luck*, pp. 210–215.

21. Pollock, M., Ketcham, C. J., Gibbon, H.M.F., Bradley, E. D., & Bata, M. (2017, October 26). Beyond the mentor-mentee model: A case for multi-mentoring in undergraduate research. *Perspectives on Undergraduate Research and Mentoring 6.1*. Retrieved from http://blogs.elon.edu/purm/2017/10/26/beyond-the-mentor-mentee-model-a-case-for-multi-mentoring-in-undergraduate-research-purm-6-1

22. Christensen, C., & Raynor, M. (2013). *The innovator's solution: Creating and sustaining successful growth*. Boston, MA: Harvard Business Review Press. These lessons in unbundling across jobs are especially powerful considering the emerging "slots" in modern school design. Integrating these slots around narrow demographics or "roles"—rather than around jobs—could end up severely limiting innovation and progress (not to mention scale). By analogy, as Christensen and Raynor pointed out in *The Innovator's Solution*, retail chains often organize their shelves and channels by product categories rather than according to the jobs that customers need to get done. This channel structure limits the extent to which innovators can orient their products on those jobs because of the need to slot products into their allocated shelf space. Schools should be wary of the same. If slots for new relationships are architected with merely a narrow category of people (e.g., "tutors") rather than a job to be done (e.g., "help me pay it forward"), they stand to attract a limited set of relationships to the system and establish exceedingly narrow roles for mentors, limiting them to a few rote transactions with students.

23. Christensen, C. M., Johnson, C. W., & Horn, M. B. (2008). *Disrupting class*. New York, NY: McGraw-Hill Professional Publishing.

24. For more on this topic, see Willingham, D. T. (2009). *Why don't students like school? A cognitive scientist answers questions about how the mind works and what it means for the classroom*. San Francisco, CA: Jossey-Bass.

25. Ibid.

26. danah boyd spells her name using all lowercase letters.

27. boyd, d. (2014). *It's complicated: The social lives of networked teens*. New Haven, CT: Yale University Press, pp. 158–167.

28. As boyd wrote, "Social media does not radically rework teens' social networks. As a result, technology does not radically reconfigure inequality. The transformative potential of the internet to restructure social networks in order to reduce structural inequality rests heavily on people's ability to leverage it to make new connections. This is not how youth use social media." boyd, *It's complicated*, 2014, p. 173.

29. The finding that many people who choose to become teachers do so because they believe they will be good at it is based on a 2015 survey of more than one thousand current teachers in England conducted by "think and action-tank" LKMco and Pearson Education. The survey's purpose was to better understand why people choose to teach and why they choose to remain in the profession. Although researchers conducted the survey in England, we believe that the results can be extrapolated to the US. In their 2015 book *Blended*, authors and education commentators Michael Horn and Heather Staker cite research from Frederick Herzberg, who wrote a widely read

Harvard Business Review article that identified achievement and recognition as the two most important "motivators" leading to job satisfaction. Horn and Staker extrapolated this finding to help explain the motivations of teachers. In his original article, Herzberg also identified ten "hygiene" factors that produce job dissatisfaction in employees. Pearson. (2015, October 23). Why teach: New research explores why people choose to go into teaching and remain there. Retrieved from https://www.pearson .com/corporate/news/media/news-announcements/2015/10/why-teach--new-research-explores-why-people-choose-to-go-into-te.html; Horn, M. B., & Staker, H. (2014). *Blended: Using disruptive innovation to improve schools.* San Francisco, CA: Jossey-Bass; Herzberg, F. (1968). One more time: How do you motivate employees? *Harvard Business Review 46*(1), 53–52. Retrieved from https://hbr.org/2003/01/one-more-time-how-do-you-motivate-employees

30. Our short list of teachers' jobs to be done is hardly exhaustive. We welcome further research into this important topic including upcoming research by our colleague Tom Arnett on why teachers hire new instructional approaches.

31. Gallup. (2016). *Gallup student poll: Engaged today—Ready for tomorrow, Fall 2015 survey results.* Retrieved from http://www.gallup.com/services/189926/student-poll-2015-results.aspx

32. Dasgupta, P. (2005). Economics of social capital. *Economic Record, 81*(s1). doi:10.1111/j.1475–4932.2005.00245.x

CHAPTER SEVEN

What Gets Measured Gets Done
School Metrics and Policies Reconsidered

Pulling Back the Curtain on Network Gaps

By traditional measures, Buckingham Browne & Nichols (BB&N) is one of the top private schools in the country. Located in Cambridge, Massachusetts, BB&N serves children from pre-K through grade 12. Tuition can stretch above $47,000 per year. BB&N's academic outcomes are impressive: students score an average of 2,100 on the SAT, and many go on to top colleges.[1]

But a few years ago, administrators at the school decided to assess BB&N's performance against a new metric: the strength of relationships between students and teachers. To do so, BB&N created "relationship maps" to identify the number of stable, positive relationships between students and adults at the school.[2] Administrators got together in a room and listed the names of each student, by grade level, on the walls. Then the administration asked faculty members to place a yellow dot next to the names of students whom they believed would approach them if they had a personal problem, and a red dot next to the names of students whom they deemed "at risk" either personally or academically.[3]

The results were surprising: some students had few yellow dots next to their names, and others had none at all. (See Figure 7.1.) Some of the students who lacked strong relationships with adults were also identified as "at risk." And still others with few positive teacher relationships were actually *high* academic performers.[4] In response, and to its great credit, BB&N took action. Administrators forged plans to better address the needs of students who may have felt disconnected. They also increased

Positive Relationship?	Student Name	At risk?
● ● ● ● ●	Michelle B.	
●	Mike S.	● ●
	Jake Z.	● ● ● ● ●

Figure 7.1 Mapping Students' Ties at School

Source: From "How-to Guide to Relationship Mapping," by Making Caring Common Project, a project of Harvard Graduate School of Education, 2017. Copyright 2017 by Harvard Graduate School of Education. Reprinted with permission. Retrieved from https://mcc.gse.harvard.edu/links/relationship-mapping

engagement from advisors, counselors, teachers, and other adults, such as sports coaches.

But the lesson was clear: traditional metrics—such as academic achievement and national rankings—masked important relationship gaps, even among some "high-performing" students.

The Power of Transparency to Drive Change

The state of students' networks remains largely invisible in our schools today. The vast majority of schools—both public and private—do not map their students' relationships in formal or frequent ways.

Making that social machinery visible is a crucial step. From there, policymakers and school leaders will no longer be able to ignore this crucial aspect of the opportunity equation.

Of course, the education system is no stranger to the effects that transparency can have in shifting policies and priorities. For example, a 1966 report called *Equality of Educational Opportunity*—better known in education circles as the *Coleman Report* for its lead author, sociologist James Coleman—sent ripples through the education establishment. Among other things, the report revealed troubling gaps in student achievement by race and class. These alarm bells grew even louder with the Reagan administration's 1983 *A Nation at Risk*, which detailed failures in America's schools. Data in these reports laid bare the shortcomings and inequalities of the public education system.

These startling statistics on poor achievement scores set into motion a series of reforms in school accountability. For policymakers, it was not enough that students were in school; what mattered was what they had to show for it. Student success and school performance began to depend on outcomes, and differences in the outcomes across student demographics.

Where do relationships fit into this relatively recent focus on academic outcomes? No school would dismiss relationships as crucial aspects of student success. But relationships themselves are typically viewed as helping *lead to* academic achievement. Even Coleman himself named students' social capital—construed at the time in a fairly narrow sense as students' family structures—as a crucial variable impacting achievement.

For better or worse, metrics drive innovation. By extension, schools will innovate along the metrics that policy prioritizes. In education, we have started down a risky path of categorizing relationships as *inputs* to narrowly construed measures of academic achievement. Instead, relationships need to ascend into the education system's view as outcomes. Like a strong track record of academic achievement, a strong and diverse network also paves the road to opportunity.

Taking Stock: Relationships as Outcomes

For any cost-conscious stakeholder accountable to short-term metrics (read: anyone in our cash-strapped education system!), it will always be tempting to value relationships, and weak ties in particular, strictly in terms of the one-off, immediate benefits they might provide. Immediate benefits, however, invite lesser investments. In lieu of a relationship, for example, an innovation could simply provide better or more targeted information to which students might not otherwise have access. We've already seen systems pivot in this direction by using automatic text messages, chatbots, and virtual reality to automate some of the benefits that weak-tie networks might otherwise offer.

It's easy to construe these "efficiencies" as equal inputs to opportunity. But doing so is a mistake. It ignores the crucial fact that social capital *can keep on giving* where one-off benefits and advice—from a pamphlet or chatbot—cannot.

Relationships Can Keep on Giving

To understand the distinction, imagine that in one scenario, a student receives a pamphlet describing best practices for navigating the college application process. If it is detailed and well written, the pamphlet could improve her chances of gaining admission to the college of her choice.

All in all, a pamphlet approach may sound like a great (and affordable!) idea. Until, that is, we consider a second scenario. Imagine the student is instead connected to a mentor charged with providing her with identical information. The student spends thirty minutes discussing the college application process with her mentor. He not only delivers the information but also answers some follow-up questions via email, provides motivational support and encouragement, and perhaps connects with her a second time to help clarify a few aspects of the process she finds confusing or opaque. Even over a short period of time, they develop a rapport with one another.

A few years later, as she's finishing up her freshman year of college, she begins to put some thought into what she might want to do after school. Although she's already spoken with her college career counselor, she wants a second opinion about what major would best support her growing aspiration to be a lawyer.

The student culls through her contacts only to recall that her high school mentor was an attorney. She reaches back out to him and schedules a time to chat. In the course of the conversation, her mentor tells her that he majored in philosophy as an undergraduate, and feels that this is a good major for lawyers because of its focus on logical reasoning. He also, however, lists several different majors that colleagues at his firm pursued.

As the conversation continues, the student also learns that if she wants to realize her dream, she should start prepping for the LSAT as early as possible. Following the call, the student purchases LSAT prep software. She and her mentor stay in touch, exchanging emails once every three or four months. A few years later, she reaches out to him again, and he connects her to a cousin of his, who's also a lawyer, to talk about law firms in Dallas, where she's hoping to work that summer.

The moral of this story? Relationships, by design, can keep giving. A pamphlet cannot.[5]

Preparing for the Unknown

Most important, if we are looking for ways to increase access to opportunity, relationships can continue to give in ways that are nearly impossible to predict ahead of time. At the time a student and a mentor, expert, or "granny" are paired together, there's no telling exactly what benefits that relationship might provide down the line. There's also no telling what might arise in a student's life—be it immense tragedy, enormous opportunity, or simply a change in career plans—that could alter her trajectory. Given these unknowns, networks are like stock portfolios or insurance policies. The stronger, broader, and deeper the reservoir of social capital a student possesses, the better equipped she is to thrive as life continuously throws new circumstances her way.

Relationships themselves, then, must be treated as an outcome if we hope that all students can take advantage of the ongoing value they stand to offer.

But for that to happen, schools and society need to understand the immense role that networks play in expanding access to opportunity, and the disparate access to networks that students face. We have some national data making this case. For example, in 2014, MENTOR, an organization that advocates for increased and effective mentorship models across the nation, released the results of the first nationally representative survey on the effects of mentorship. Among other findings, MENTOR reported that at-risk youth who had a mentor were substantially more likely to both aspire to, and enroll in, college.[6] Meanwhile, in his 2015 book *Our Kids: The American Dream in Crisis,* Harvard professor Robert Putnam painted a sweeping portrait of rising inequality in students' social connections and decreasing rates of upward mobility. Combining quantitative research with qualitative interviews profiling young people from a variety of backgrounds, *Our Kids* represented a noteworthy effort to shed light on emerging opportunity gaps.[7]

These, however, are just the beginning of filling in our knowledge base on the state of students' networks. More and better data could function much as achievement data did in national education reforms of the second half of the twentieth century: it could spur a system-wide response to tackling opportunity gaps that currently exist but remain hidden or anecdotal at best.

How Schools Can Measure Webs of Relationships over Time

Not all schools have the deep pockets of elite private schools to dedicate to relationship mapping. But the simple act of assessing students' access to relationships can occur in any school, as examples like City Connects, described in chapter 3, illustrate. Luckily, new measurement strategies are emerging that could help schools take this leap.

Before schools take action, they must figure out how to measure relationships at the "unit" of the student. Given widespread use of traditional metrics, many teachers and administrators may struggle with where to start. We empathize: none of the schools that we attended, from kindergarten through graduate school, were measuring the relationships that we possessed or built over time with teachers, peers, or adults beyond the building. The evolution of those networks was effectively left to chance.

Fortunately, taking stock of the contours of student networks is not as difficult as it may seem. Tools and practices abound, and some schools are already arriving at social capital metrics, either accidentally or deliberately.

Evolving measures tend to focus on the scope, strength, utility, and diversity of students' networks.

We have already touched on the promising practice of relationship mapping, which BB&N successfully used to make the invisible visible. Developed by researchers at the Harvard Graduate School of Education's Making Caring Common Project, relationship mapping can help schools adjust their practices to effectively forge trusting relationships between students and adults. (See Figure 7.1.) All it takes is a room with student names and a healthy supply of yellow and red stickers. Although BB&N's relatively small size allowed administrators to map all students at once, larger schools may prefer to move through the process one grade level at a time.[8] From there, schools that identify students who lack trusting relationships with adults can direct more connections and resources accordingly.

To holistically assess the full range of relationships in students' lives, including those outside school, schools should also look to best practices among social workers. For decades, social workers have used asset mapping to assess the support networks of their clients. One example is the

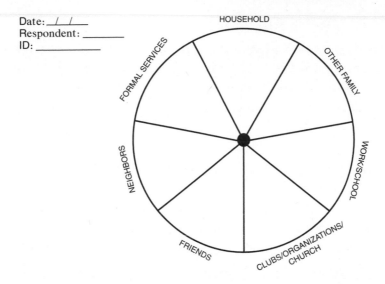

Date: __/__/__
Respondent: _____
ID: _____

HOUSEHOLD
OTHER FAMILY
WORK/SCHOOL
CLUBS/ORGANIZATIONS/ CHURCH
FRIENDS
NEIGHBORS
FORMAL SERVICES

Figure 7.2 Social Network Mapping

Source: From "The Social Network Map: Assessing Social Support in Clinical Practice," by Elizabeth M. Tracy and James K. Whittaker, October 1990, *Journal of Contemporary Human Services.* Reprinted with permission from *Families in Society* (www.familiesinsociety .org), published by the Alliance for Strong Families and Communities.

Social Network Map, developed by researchers Elizabeth Tracy of Case Western Reserve University and James Whittaker of the University of Washington. (See Figure 7.2.) The tool helps identify and sort the structure and quality of a client's support system by mapping relationships into several categories, including family, friends and coworkers.[9]

This may sound labor intensive. Luckily, however, although some of the metrics and measurement tools we've described are paper based, technology tools are starting to emerge that can streamline and grow these efforts exponentially.

For example, mobile applications such as the Patient Centered Network App have emerged in health care circles to help providers map out the various supports in patients' lives and then connect them to local resources. Using the app, providers can map existing assets and relationships in patients' lives, including the strength and importance of those ties. Educators are now piloting this same tool in school settings. By asking students or parents questions such as "Where do you already get support?"

"Are you connected to others that can support you?" and "Are those people connected to one another?" the app effectively assesses individuals' and families' personal support networks and identifies gaps in social support needs. In circumstances where this is integrated into an existing network of care, the app then taps into databases of service providers to generate customized referrals to link people to community resources.[10]

Tools like these are especially exciting in their potential to unlock and coordinate the existing *assets* in students' lives. By beginning with a map of existing ties in students' lives—many of which teachers or school officials may simply not have been aware of—schools can more deliberately tap those resources in a more systematic manner.

From there, schools interested in diversifying student networks could add to these maps through simple "name generator" exercises. These could enable schools to generate data on students' access to informal mentors, as cited in chapter 1. For example, by asking students "Do you know an engineer? . . . a lawyer? . . . a salesperson?" schools could surface additional assets in students' lives, while also revealing gaps in their current exposure to particular industries or demographics. From there, schools could target access to internships and experts accordingly—to both address gaps and targets students' interests and passions.

Of course, mapping relationships should also be done in the context of developmental phases of students' lives and measures of quality at each phase. The networks of a first-grader and of a junior in high school will likely look radically different.

To account for these differences, schools can adopt measures that are sensitive to the different phases and progression of a given relationship. One compelling research-based example of this is the Search Institute's Developmental Relationships Framework. The framework can help schools track and evaluate a student-mentor or student-teacher relationship's healthy progression over time—from phases such as "getting to know each other" to "building mutual trust" all the way to "confirming shared commitments" and "investing in each other's growth."[11]

As described in chapter 5, as more "slots" or pathways in the education system begin to open up, schools can also start to measure the extent to which exposure to experiences beyond the four walls of school increases the size of a student's network—and if and how those relationships persist and flourish. Doing so could enable schools to start to identify the ongoing *utility* of that network. Some Big Picture Learning schools, for example, track how often relationships between students and their mentors at their internship sites lead to opportunities down the line. According to the organization's own research with MPR Associates, at three of their schools in California, an impressive 74 percent of their high school graduates who were working (and not in school) were able to obtain employment through contacts made during their high school internships.[12]

Measurement Approaches for System Leaders and Policymakers

Efforts like these could help schools surface and address social capital gaps *within* schools. But in order to address the issue of student networks *systemically*, policymakers and leaders will have to adopt measures that provide insights *across* schools, demographics, and regions.

Although it may be difficult to measure young people's social capital at scale, it is not impossible. In fact, efforts are already afoot. One of the most comprehensive efforts hails from America's Promise Alliance, a Washington, DC–based nonprofit focused on improving the lives of America's youth, which has long advocated for closing gaps in students' access to "caring adults." Working with such partners as the Search Institute, Gallup, and Child Trends, America's Promise Alliance's Center for Promise research group has continued to reveal substantial disparities in young people's access to caring adults. Specifically, a 2006 study showed that young people from low-income backgrounds ages twelve to seventeen were 10 percentage points less likely than their high-income peers to have caring adults in their lives.[13] Racial disparities in social capital also surfaced in the research: another 2006 study showed that 53 percent of African Americans ages eight to twenty-one said that they "wish they had more adults they could turn to when they need help," compared to 38 percent of whites from the same age demographic.[14] Since then, researchers at the Center for Promise have also investigated the adult-to-youth ratio across various neighborhoods, and the effect these ratios appear to have on graduation rates. Among other findings, mapping neighborhoods in their sample revealed that "a 1 percent increase in the adult-to-youth ratio results in a 1 percent decrease in the rate of young people leaving school. In real-world terms, this result means that for every seven more adults in the neighborhood, one fewer young person leaves school."[15] System leaders and policymakers can begin to use research like this as a barometer for gauging the state of young people's strong-tie networks in their cities and states.

There is also emerging *international* data that could help leaders compare the health of student networks among different countries. In 2017, the Programme for International Student Assessment (PISA) published its first-ever study on student "well-being," defined as "the psychological, cognitive, social and physical functioning and capabilities that students need to live a happy and fulfilling life."[16] Although the study did not focus exclusively on relationships, it surfaced country-level data on the "percentage of students who reported talking to their parents after school" and the percentage of students "who agreed/strongly agreed with the following statement: 'My parents support me when I am facing difficulties at school.'" For systems, measures like these could offer useful proxies for the strength of relationships between young people and their parents.[17] One could imagine PISA adding similar questions about relationships to peers and mentors so as to eventually offer a fuller picture of the health of students' networks.

More data points like these can serve as a good anchor or baseline for an improved understanding of social capital disparities by the *number* and to some degree the *strength* of ties in students' lives. But eventually system leaders will need to move beyond counting single nodes of care or trust, such as parents, teachers, and mentors. To best approximate networks of opportunity, these metrics need to go even further, to calibrate the *diversity* of ties in students' lives.

In other words, policymakers and system leaders must figure out ways to capture the depth and breadth of student networks. Here, social network analysis tools may prove useful. These tools visually map patterns of human connection, and have developed substantially over the last decade or so in applications as diverse as marketing and counterterrorism. System leaders could embark on regional or statewide mapping exercises to understand the social networks that govern access to the knowledge economy, as well as the social connections that could be leveraged to better network students from low-income families into high-paying sectors.

In short, to create demand for solutions that tackle the social side of opportunity gaps, we'll need even more data in order to better understand both the gravity and nuances of the social capital gaps before us. Once we have it, data like this could translate into intentional efforts to redistribute or target funds through methods such as means-testing for students' access to relationships (to determine those eligible for additional supports or subsidies) in the same manner that we currently means-test by family income to determine school-based subsidies. These efforts could in turn move broader funding structures beyond program-level mentoring and education funds to integrated dollars dedicated to addressing gaps in access to opportunity writ large.

Enabling Conditions—Policies That Will Open Up Schools and Ensure Safety

Large-scale efforts to measure students' access to networks of support and opportunity could send waves through an education system that currently optimizes for what students know, but largely ignores whom they know. By beginning to measure relationships as a salient variable shaping opportunity, policymakers could urge school systems to integrate this missing half of the opportunity equation into their models.

But policymakers' efforts shouldn't end there. As with any systems change, simply measuring the state of students' networks does not equip schools with the resources, tools, or conditions to actually address network gaps. And even for schools willing to make this leap, policies that reinforce traditional school structures might hold them back.

To become caring and networking hubs, schools will need to operate under policies that break open historical constraints on where students can learn and from whom, and when that learning takes place. It will also require continued—if not far greater—investment in mentoring programs and community-based efforts to strengthen and expand young people's networks. Finally, these efforts to open up networks must be constantly and vigilantly accompanied by clear privacy and safety guidelines that

protect students from bad actors who might exploit a more open architecture of school.

Policies will likely emerge as examples such as Summit, VLACS, and
City Connects mature. From an innovation theory perspective, it is hardly
surprising that many of today's education policies are not fully caught up
to realizing the potential of these innovative models. Policy often follows—
rather than catalyzes—the earliest stages of disruptive innovations.[18] But
innovations are starting to push the system to consider new policies that
loosen historical restrictions on when or how students learn.

Extended Learning Opportunities

One oft-ignored policy innovation has started to take root, tugging on the
strong gravitational pull of schools' closed-off, insular traditions: extended
learning opportunities (ELOs).

An ELO—albeit a broad concept—tends to refer to a credit-bearing
activity that takes place outside a traditional, in-school academic course.
Take one concrete example: in New Hampshire, an ELO is defined as "the
primary acquisition of knowledge and skills through instruction or study
outside of the traditional classroom methodology, including, but not
limited to, apprenticeships, community service, independent study, online
courses, internships, performing groups, and private instruction."[19]

As described in chapter 5, New Hampshire's own Virtual Learning
Academy Charter School (VLACS) is pursuing one of the most exciting
experiments in these sorts of opportunities. The traditionally fully online
institution has spent the past few years developing three- to four-week
projects that allow students to engage in real-world settings in order to
earn credits against competencies. This work is assessed by an online
teacher-of-record through a series of performance assessments that the
organization has developed. In other words, through ELO policies, schools
can become looser on *how* and *where* a student learns, while still remaining
tight on assessing the outcomes of that learning.

This effort, however, is not merely the result of the state's innovative
policy permitting schools to award credit for coursework outside traditional classrooms. Steve Kossakoski, the current head of VLACS, insists
that ELOs can't function as a stand-alone effort, but must go hand in hand

with a competency-based approach that breaks down courses into more discrete modules that can be mastered either in a traditional class or through outside experiences. "An ELO policy in a state without the option to meet course requirements through competencies would be quite restrictive," Kossakoski said. "For example, a student working in a hospital may be able to master certain competencies in biology, but probably not the full set of competencies found in a typical high school biology course. In this case a school might award a generic elective credit or no credit at all and the student would still be required to take a traditional biology course."[20]

In other words, so long as schools measure credits at the level of entire courses, traditional instructional models will dominate traditional coursework. Instead, in Kossakoski's experience, being able to break down a biology course into competencies allows the student to master competencies in different learning environments (for example, internships, courses, independent learning experiences). Breaking down coursework in this manner also means that a single ELO experience could count toward credit across multiple disciplines. For example, a student participating in an internship in a hospital might end up completing competencies in biology and English, depending on the type of assigned duties or projects.

Competency-Based Learning Policies

It's not surprising then that as VLACS develops industry-embedded projects, it is simultaneously in the process of changing its own academic terminology from "courses" to "competency groups" or "bundles." For VLACS, like many school systems trying to open up learning beyond the four walls of school, this involves rethinking all the ways in which students might learn and then making those experiences sufficiently flexible and interchangeable, with strong assessments to ensure rigor.

Luckily, a movement to make this viable is already under way. Numerous state and federal policymakers are increasingly embracing *competency-based learning.* In a competency-based system, students advance upon demonstrating mastery. This model marks a sharp departure from the school system's traditional metric: hours spent in the classroom.

According to the national nonprofit CompetencyWorks, a high-quality competency-based model is one in which

1. Students advance upon demonstrated mastery.
2. Competencies include explicit, measurable, transferable learning objectives that empower students.
3. Assessment is meaningful and a positive learning experience for students.
4. Students receive rapid, differentiated support based on their individual learning needs.
5. Learning outcomes emphasize competencies that include application and creation of knowledge along with the development of important skills and dispositions.[21]

Each of these tenets of a competency-based system requires dramatic changes to traditional teaching and learning. From a policy perspective, however, moving to such a system means reconsidering how schools *account* for learning—which historically has been inextricable from time.

At the turn of the twentieth century, in an effort to standardize high school curricula and college admissions, a committee at the National Education Association determined that a satisfactory year's work in a given high school subject would require no fewer than 120 one-hour instructional periods. This became known as the "Carnegie unit," or credit unit. To this day, graduating high school still hinges on accumulating such credits. As a result, school policies end up emphasizing credit hours as much as measuring actual learning. So long as a student logs the necessary hours and receives at least a passing grade, he can move on to the next course. And in many schools, grades may draw on factors like attendance, extra credit, and good behavior, rather than demonstration of mastery.

Today, however, the Carnegie unit is showing its age. Time-based measures leave students susceptible to moving on to material before they are ready, or remaining mired in a subject they have already mastered.

In addition to introducing flexible pacing, competency-based education attempts to import newfound rigor to the concept of "mastery." In this new system, "competencies" describe what students should know, as well as what they should be able to do. Competency-based assessments aim to test students' ability to demonstrate what they can do in real-world applications and across a variety of contexts.

For the purposes of nurturing and expanding networks, competency-based models stand to unlock flexibilities that would allow more schools to operate like VLACS, awarding credit for out-of-school experiences that simultaneously enrich students' networks. These policies can also begin to unlock more flexible approaches to assessment: beyond traditional paper-and-pencil tests, students could begin to receive authentic feedback from adults working in a given industry to certify their learning—which could function as both a check on learning and a check on the quality of a students' relationship with a given mentor or expert. Finally, high-quality competency-based models require robust "just-in-time" supports for students. In a networked school model, this support could eventually hail from a variety of sources, including a mix of teachers, online tutors, or even Mitra's "grannies."

Privacy and Infrastructure Policies to Secure Students' Networks

Extended learning opportunities and competency-based credit policies can lift regulatory barriers to where, when, and how students earn credit. These policies can in turn allow for a more open architecture of school that facilitates broader networks across students' experiences.

That said, this open architecture is not without challenges and risks. These risks are especially high as they pertain to protecting students. Privacy and safety policies will need to evolve. Schools and policymakers must update privacy policies to ensure that connections occur in a safe and secure manner, without being so stringent as to inadvertently isolate students from relationships with supportive mentors, coaches, or experts.

In part, this will hinge on schools themselves ensuring that the right technological and educational resources are in place. Along with internet filters and appropriate background check and visitor policies, schools should offer internet safety education to their students.[22] Further, when contracting with third-party tools like those described in previous chapters, schools can demand that these providers follow clear and reliable safety measures. For online interactions in particular, schools could stipulate that programs put rigorous oversight mechanisms in place. For example, they could require that tools include features such as iCouldBe's proprietary software that monitors for any potentially inappropriate communication. Software should also prevent users from accessing one another's location. Design features like these can help ensure that connections are safe and secure—without preventing them from occurring in the first place.

These safety precautions will be far more feasible, however, if policies are in place that allow existing security and safety systems to talk to one another. For example, according to MENTOR's research, currently "only half of states provide access to national FBI fingerprint checks to mentoring programs and other youth-serving organizations. Programs without access are left to choose between often costly screenings offered through private companies or skip a national FBI fingerprint check altogether." Policies that would expand access to existing background check information would enable more schools and mentoring programs to process background checks efficiently and reliably.[23]

Policy efforts focused on safety will need to be paired with tools and policies focused on infrastructure. The logistics alone of networking students in new ways could easily prove too overwhelming for a traditional school to coordinate.

Technology tools could play an important role in addressing some of these challenges. First, organizational and scheduling tools that streamline the logistics of the new anytime, anywhere, anyone opportunities could alleviate significant burdens for schools trying to coordinate ELOs. And platforms that supply a range of online experts may provide scalable solutions to furnishing students with diverse real-world experiences, even in geographies with a limited supply of face-to-face internships, job shadow opportunities, or community-based projects.

That said, policies should also be in place to ease some of the logistical struggles. For example, transportation policies could subsidize student access to low-cost or free transportation to and from out-of-school learning experiences or internships. Investing in robust digital infrastructure will help too. Policies that support bringing fiber and Wi-Fi into schools will be crucial precursors to enabling schools to take advantage of network-enhancing tools, especially those that facilitate video chats between students and remote mentors or experts. Particularly as networking tools continue to grow, this basic infrastructure will need to be in place so that all students—

especially those in remote or resource-constrained environments, can make use of disruptive tools.[24]

A Relationship-Rich Future

Innovations in school design and disruptive technologies are making the possibility of a highly networked school a reality. For these innovations to take root and spread, measurement and policy will need to nurture and guide them. By treating relationships as a twenty-first-century asset for all students, schools and policymakers can begin to prioritize this crucial half of the opportunity equation—and address relationship gaps once and for all.

KEY TAKEAWAYS

- Few schools employ deliberate, ongoing efforts to measure student networks—neither within nor beyond school. However, tools that could help schools do so are beginning to emerge.
- A holistic measurement agenda—within and across school systems—will be crucial to bringing relationship and opportunity gaps to the fore of school design. Much as the *Coleman Report* and *A Nation at Risk* lent transparency to troubling achievement gaps, better data on students' networks can awaken school systems and policymakers alike to social capital gaps.
- From there, schools can begin to use promising approaches to measurement—ones that draw on the wisdom of tools such as social worker network maps, online networking platforms, and social networking analysis—to better gauge the strength, diversity, and quality of their students' networks over time.
- Looking ahead, policymakers will need to attend to other policy levers—such as how schools measure and award credit, investments in robust transportation and digital infrastructure, and reliable privacy and safety policies—to ensure that schools are able to meaningfully and securely open up to the outside world in order to strengthen and expand their students' networks over time.

Notes

1. Martin, E. (2016, March 10). The 50 best private high schools in America. *Business Insider*. Retrieved from http://www.businessinsider.com/best-private-high-schools-in-america-2016-3/#19-buckingham-browne-and-nichols-school-32

2. Making Caring Common Project. (2017). How-to guide to relationship mapping. Harvard Graduate School of Education. Retrieved from https://mcc.gse.harvard.edu/files/gse-mcc/files/relationship_mapping_pitch_and_guide_0_0.pdf

3. The red dots identifying "at risk" students and the yellow dots identifying a strong relationship with a teacher were not mutually exclusive; a student's name could have both kinds of dots next to it. Making Caring Common Project, a project of Harvard Graduate School of Education, How-to guide to relationship mapping.

4. Ibid.

5. Freeland Fisher, J. (2017, July 7). Why chatbots make me nervous [Web log post]. Retrieved from https://www.christenseninstitute.org/blog/chatbots-make-nervous

6. Bruce, M., & Bridgeland, J. (2014). The mentoring effect: Young people's perspectives on the outcomes and availability of mentoring. Retrieved from https://files.eric.ed.gov/fulltext/ED558065.pdf

7. Putnam, R. D. (2015). *Our kids: The American dream in crisis*. New York, NY: Simon & Schuster.

8. Making Caring Common Project, How-to guide to relationship mapping.

9. Tracy, E. M., & Whittaker, J. K. (1990). The social network map: Assessing social support in clinical practice. *Families in Society: The Journal of Contemporary Social Services, 71*(8), 461–470.

10. Center on Network Science. (n.d.). What is the person-centered care app? Retrieved from http://partnertool.net/tools-and-training/pcn-app; Center on Network Science. (n.d.). Who can use the PCN app? Retrieved from http://partnertool.net/wp-content/uploads/2016/09/PCN-Brochure.pdf

11. Roehlkepartain, E., Pekel, K., Syvertsen, A., Sethi, J., Sullivan, T., & Scales, P. (2017). Relationships first: Creating connections that help young people thrive [Web log post]. Retrieved from http://www.search-institute.org/blog/new-research-report

12. The 74 percent figure represents a rough estimate, and refers to an alumni survey of three Big Picture Schools in California (Met Sacramento, Met West, and San Diego Met). One major limitation of the survey was the relatively small number of respondents: although the response rate at Met West met the 70 percent threshold considered sufficient for general extrapolation, response rates at the other two schools did not. Nonetheless, the point here is not to adjudicate the finding. Rather, it is to emphasize that the metric itself (percentage of graduates working and not in college who obtained employment as a result of contacts made during their high school internships) is a good way to measure the utility of student networks that arise out of school design. MPR Associates. (2012). *Big Picture Learning: High school alumni report*. Retrieved from https://1.cdn.edl.io/vGIpPEdMJfGhhJdIeQYfWT5OJ1oR2YyyjCgWLjqrqpaG8rLt.pdf

13. America's Promise Alliance. (2006). Every child, every promise: Turning failure into action. Retrieved from https://eric.ed.gov/?id=ED505358. Original report: Scales, P. C., Benson, P. L., Bartig, K., Streit, K., Moore, K. A., Lippman, L., . . . Theokas, C. (2006, April). Keeping America's promises to children and youth: A Search Institute-Child Trends report on the results of the America's Promise national telephone polls

of children, teenagers, and parents. Retrieved from https://www.childtrends.org/wp-content/uploads/2006/04/CChild_Trends-2010_08_25-FR_EducPromises.pdf

14. America's Promise Alliance, Every child, every promise.

15. America's Promise Alliance. (2016). Who's minding the neighborhood? Retrieved from http://www.americaspromise.org/sites/default/files/d8/AdultCapacity_ResearchBrief_final_0.pdf. This report is based on an econometric study conducted in 2016 by Thomas Malone and Dr. Jonathan Zaff.

16. OECD. (2017). *PISA 2015 results (Volume III): Students' well-being.* Paris, France: OECD Publishing. doi:10.1787/9789264273856-en

17. Ibid.

18. Here, the business world provides instructive examples. Southwest Airlines, for instance, started by offering short routes within its home state of Texas. By flying only within state lines, Southwest was literally and figuratively flying under the radar of interstate federal regulation—which afforded the company flexibilities that could keep prices down. Over time, low-cost regional carriers like Southwest showed regulators that a new cost structure did not threaten passenger safety. This in turn opened the door to loosening regulations on airfare that had kept ticket prices much higher among mainstream airline companies. Southwest's example accelerated the collapse of certain federal aviation regulations, allowing Southwest and other low-cost carriers to expand their services to increasingly longer routes, pressuring and eventually disrupting incumbent carriers for whom the lower-margin shorter routes were initially unattractive. For more on the relationship between disruption and deregulation, see Christensen, C. M., Grossman, J. H., & Hwang, J. (2009). *The innovator's prescription: A disruptive solution for health care.* New York, NY: McGraw Hill.

19. New Hampshire Department of Education. (n.d.). Extended learning opportunities. Retrieved from https://www.education.nh.gov/innovations/elo

20. Freeland Fisher, J. (2015, April 22). Anytime, anywhere, anyone: How far can we extend extended learning opportunities? [Web log post]. Retrieved from https://www.christenseninstitute.org/blog/anytime-anywhere-anyone-how-far-can-we-extend-extended-learning-opportunities

21. CompetencyWorks. (n.d.). What is competency education? Retrieved from https://www.competencyworks.org/about/competency-education

22. See for example, the National Cyber Security Alliance resources at https://staysafeonline.org/

23. MENTOR. (n.d.). Child safety. Retrieved from http://www.mentoring.org/child-safety

24. The nonprofit Education SuperHighway provides comprehensive data on school connectivity across the country. The organization hopes that by 2020, all students will attend schools with internet speeds necessary to take advantage of digital learning and educational opportunity. Yet as of 2017, 2,049 schools across the country still needed high-speed fiber connections; 77 percent of these schools are in rural communities. Another ten thousand schools still lack sufficient Wi-Fi. Education SuperHighway. (2017). *2017 state of the states: Fulfilling our promise to America's students.* Retrieved from https://stateofthestates.educationsuperhighway.org

CONCLUSION

Designing for a Networked Society, Labor Market, and Life

Zuckerberg Goes Analog

At the start of 2017, Facebook founder Mark Zuckerberg posted a heartfelt note to his eighty million online followers. As part of his New Year's resolution, he vowed to spend the next year traveling to talk to people in every state.

> Going into this challenge, it seems we are at a turning point in history. For decades, technology and globalization have made us more productive and connected. This has created many benefits, but for a lot of people it has also made life more challenging. This has contributed to a greater sense of division than I have felt in my lifetime. We need to find a way to change the game so it works for everyone. My work is about connecting the world and giving everyone a voice. I want to personally hear more of those voices this year . . . My trips this year will take different forms—road trips with Priscilla, stops in small towns and universities, visits to our offices across the country, meetings with teachers and scientists, and trips to fun places you recommend along the way.[1]

The irony of Zuckerberg's challenge, of course, cannot be understated. One of the world's leading social networking entrepreneurs wants to go meet with people *in person*? By *car*? He might as well have said he'd be riding a covered wagon from Silicon Valley back across the plains.

Whether Zuckerberg intended it or not, his resolution posed a paradox that is core to our social lives in the twenty-first century. Today, innovations that connect people abound. Networking apps, online dating sites, and high-speed communications are part of daily life. Internet connectivity is at an all-time high. And most teachers can attest to the fact that young people of all ages are more "connected"—technologically speaking—than ever.

Yet amid this marvelous progress, we remain stubbornly separated. Class, race, geography, and belief systems continue to divide us. In many ways, we feel less connected, not more. Where seemingly fundamental or intractable differences exist, we can hardly manage to see one another. Children, of course, are not immune to these trends. They inherit their parents' social networks—networks that are mirrored and reinforced by the neighborhoods and geographies in which they live and the schools they attend.

Technology could serve as an antidote to these trends. It makes forging and maintain connections vastly easier for us. But up until now, by and large people have used technology such as Facebook to reinforce their offline networks, not to wholly reinvent them. It's not surprising, then, that to reach out beyond his *existing* networks in a meaningful way, Zuckerberg needed to seek out something more than high-speed internet and an online profile. He needed to pursue a different sort of innovation—one that would put him face-to-face with those he otherwise wouldn't meet. He needed to take to the road.

America itself may be in need of such a road trip. Troubling patterns are straining the fabric of our society. Particularly, older Americans are reporting profound—and by some accounts increasing—levels of loneliness. Former US surgeon general Vivek Murthy has even gone so far as to declare that Americans are suffering a "loneliness epidemic."[2]

Yet even amid this sense of isolation, Americans also appear to be getting even *pickier* about whom they mingle with and live among. In what writer Bill Bishop has dubbed "The Big Sort," stark geographic and political divides are emerging. Democrats and Republicans now live further apart than ever.[3]

In other words, we are voluntarily Balkanizing into more insular communities and simultaneously becoming more lonely.[4] Trends like these raise difficult questions. What kind of world will our children inherit? How well will they be able to connect and relate to the people in it?

Through no inherent fault of their own, schools risk inadvertently exacerbating the situation. To correct course, they will need to take a page from Zuckerberg's book of resolutions. They will need to explore new channels—or slots—by which supportive and diverse relationships become part of their designs. They will need to adopt a new architecture better suited to offering caring, deeper relationships when students lack access to those supports at home. They will need to embrace innovations to reach outside their buildings, in ways that expand rather than merely reinforce networks. In short, they will need to find ways to operate that cut through the profound disconnects and inequalities emerging in our society. By doing so, schools have the chance to at once address troubling holes in our social fabric and to level the playing field of opportunity.

Luckily, the designs and tools described in this book are beginning to bring this within reach. Schools are entering an era when they can become networking and caring hubs.

Schools' Role in a Networked Future

Many—from John Dewey to Donald Trump—would agree that schools have a meaningful role to play in tackling these broader trends facing society. As inequality has plagued the country, there have been calls from both sides of the aisle for better schools that can help level the playing field. This book joins those calls.

But it bears noting that others have argued that against the backdrop of harsh inequality, schools actually matter *less*. Take a 2017 study by UC Berkeley economist Jesse Rothstein. Rothstein studied several national surveys in an effort to determine the effects of school quality on social mobility. He found scant evidence that variations in school quality drove variation in intergenerational mobility. Instead, he hypothesized, other factors and institutions play a greater role in children's access to opportunity. He identified "job networks or the structure of the local labor and marriage markets, rather than the education system, as likely factors influencing intergenerational economic mobility."[5]

The study was met with more than a little controversy in education reform circles. Journalists reporting on Rothstein's findings were quick to pen headlines dismissing schools as engines for social mobility. But the research can be read in another light. His findings need not be a testament to schools' looming irrelevance. Rather, they tell us more about how schools today need to be designed in order to successfully tackle non-academic gaps that shape access to opportunity.

Schools are institutions that can, if designed to do so, broker the sorts of social capital that Rothstein cites as driving social mobility. The real question that research like Rothstein's begs of education systems is how they might begin to merge academic, social, and community factors into a coherent institution that *does* pave the way to opportunity.

Shifting Social Capital to Match Our Needs

The relationships that students could benefit from, of course, may evolve over time for personal or economic reasons. Social capital is not necessarily a fixed asset. The value of a given relationship can shift depending on circumstances. In fact, as economies change, existing stocks of social capital can actually hinder rather than help people. For example, Sweden's strong social capital in the industrial steel era has had a hard time changing to support the country's new knowledge economy. The whole community revolved around one form of social capital. Since then, workers have needed to embrace greater diversity and tolerance in their networks to transition to a new economy.[6]

It follows that the role of schools—as gatekeepers to personal and professional opportunities and networks—will likely need to shift with local and national labor markets.

But there is little to suggest that relationships will cease to matter, or that social skills and connections will not command a premium. In fact, the labor market *increasingly* rewards social skills. From 1980 and 2012, jobs requiring "high levels of social interaction" grew by almost 12 percent, while less social jobs shrank.[7]

Social connections are also likely to matter more as the future of work rapidly shifts in the age of automation. Many predict that the lifespan of discrete skill sets and jobs will dramatically decrease. In the face of these shifts, nimble and diverse networks will become crucial assets. According to Deloitte's Future of Work experts, "Individuals will need to find others who can help them get better faster—small workgroups, organizations, and broader and more diverse social networks." Looking ahead at these trends, they anticipate "much richer and more diverse forms of collaboration" permeating the workforce.[8]

There is even less evidence to suggest that relationships will cease to matter in our personal lives. In arguably *the* landmark longitudinal studies on adult development, known as the Grant and Glueck studies, relationships—more than any other variable—predicted subjects' happiness and health as they aged. Harvard professor of psychiatry Robert Waldinger, who directed the study, summed it up: "When we gathered together everything we knew about them about at age 50, it wasn't their middle-age cholesterol levels that predicted how they were going to grow old. It was how satisfied they were in their relationships. The people who were the most satisfied in their relationships at age 50 were the healthiest at age 80."[9] These findings spanned a sample of Harvard graduates and individuals living in the inner city. They also spanned time, including the shift from an industrial to a knowledge economy that America has undergone over the last half a century. Relationships remained deeply relevant throughout.

Schools are no stranger to the special power of relationships. They deal in that power every day. But the exciting opportunity ahead is that innovations can double down on the power of relationships in students' lives. Schools can invest in instructional models that deepen teacher-student relationships; they can integrate student support models that enrich students' strongest-tie networks; and they can deploy emerging technologies that expand students' acquaintanceship networks to new corners of the world. These innovations stand to shape the next phase of school as we know it.

Over the course of writing this book, we were struck by how often we came back again and again to two core principles. First, opportunity is social. Achievement may be seen as a proxy for individual merit, but our ability to survive and thrive hinges on social connectedness.

Second, schools are institutions that have been designed. Our systems—from our meritocracy to our neighborhoods to our online tools and, of course, to our schools—are man-made. They can be man-unmade too. The designs of these institutions are not fixed. But they stand to fix the fates of the students they serve. And with the right innovations, they stand to help equality of opportunity—and specifically access to diverse and powerful networks—become a reality for more young people.

Franklin D. Roosevelt once wrote, "If civilization is to survive, we must cultivate the science of human relationships—the ability of all peoples, of all kinds, to live together, in the same world at peace."[10] Statistics on our social lives and the social lives of our children are too stark to ignore. Our students' networks will serve as their reservoir of connections that help them get ahead and their net of connections that help them get by and thrive. Schools are at a turning point: they can innovate in ways that promise to fill that reservoir and weave that net.

Notes

1. Zuckerberg, M. (2017, January 3). [Facebook post]. Retrieved from https://www.facebook.com/zuck/posts/10103385178272401
2. Hafner, K. (2016, September 6). Researchers confront epidemic of loneliness. *New York Times*. Retrieved from https://www.nytimes.com/2016/09/06/health/lonliness-aging-health-effects.html. According to John Cacioppo, leading researcher on loneliness, "The longest subsample is the Health and Retirement Study in the United States. That's a study the federal government has been running for decades now, and those are the data I base our own estimates on. When we look at that survey, it looks like loneliness is around 27, 28 percent. Our best estimates based on that means it's increased anywhere on the order of 3 to 7 percent over the last 20 years." Khazan, O. (2017, April 6). How loneliness begets loneliness. *Atlantic*. Retrieved from https://www.theatlantic.com/health/archive/2017/04/how-loneliness-begets-loneliness/521841/; Murthy, V. (2017, September). Work and the loneliness epidemic. *Harvard Business Review*. Retrieved from https://hbr.org/cover-story/2017/09/work-and-the-loneliness-epidemic
3. Bishop, B. (2009). *The big sort: Why the clustering of like-minded America is tearing us apart*. New York, NY: Houghton Mifflin Harcourt.
4. For a compelling discussion of these twin phenomena, see Brown, B. (2017). *Braving the wilderness: The quest for true belonging and the courage to stand alone*. New York, NY: Random House.
5. Rothstein, J. (2016). *Inequality of educational opportunity? Schools as mediators of the intergenerational transmission of income* (University of California, Berkeley and NBER

Working Paper). Retrieved from https://eml.berkeley.edu/~jrothst/workingpapers/rothstein_mobility_april2017.pdf

6. Westlund, H. (2004). *Social capital, innovation policy and the emergence of the knowledge society: A comparison between Sweden, Japan and the USA.* Retrieved from https://www.tillvaxtanalys.se/download/18.6a3ab2f1525cf0f4f95eb8e/1453901727615

7. Deming, D. (2015). *The growing importance of social skills in the labor market* (NBER Working Paper No. 21473). doi:10.3386/w21473

8. Hagel, J., Schwartz, J., & Bersin, J. (2017, July 31). Navigating the future of work: Can we point business, workers, and social institutions in the same direction? *Deloitte Review,* (21). Retrieved from https://www2.deloitte.com/content/dam/insights/us/collections/issue-21/Deloitte-Review-Issue21.pdf

9. Waldinger, R. (2015, November). What makes a good life? Lessons from the longest study on happiness [Video file]. Retrieved from https://www.ted.com/talks/robert_waldinger_what_makes_a_good_life_lessons_from_the_longest_study_on_happiness

10. Roosevelt, F. D. (1945, April 13). Undelivered address prepared for Jefferson Day. Retrieved from http://www.presidency.ucsb.edu/ws/?pid=16602

ABOUT THE AUTHORS

Julia Freeland Fisher has worked in education innovation for over a decade. She is currently director of education research at the Clayton Christensen Institute, a nonprofit, nonpartisan think tank. She leads a team devoted to informing policymakers and community leaders on the power of disruptive innovation to transform schools. Her writing has appeared in outlets including CNN, *Education Next, Forbes,* entrepreneur .com, the *Chicago Sun-Times,* and the *New Hampshire Union Leader.*

■ ■ ■

Daniel Fisher served as an infantry and scout platoon leader in the US Army, deploying to Afghanistan from 2011–2012. He was later a veterans' affairs field representative for Congressman Joe Courtney (CT-02). He currently works as a subject matter expert for the US government.

ACKNOWLEDGMENTS

THIS IS A BOOK ABOUT THE POWER OF RELATIONSHIPS. ONE OF THE THINGS THAT PROMPTED me to research this topic is my own limitless gratitude for the many people who have inspired, advised, pushed, cared for, and encouraged me professionally and personally.

To the team at the Clayton Christensen Institute, thank you for your tireless work to unpack the potential of game-changing innovations, and your feedback on big ideas. Thank you to Jenny White, Tom Arnett, Luis Flores, Alana Dunagan, Richard Price, Cliff Maxwell, and Audrey Hall for your contributions to our research. Thank you especially to Ann Christensen for supporting this work. Thank you to Hayden Hill for your incredible friendship and for encouraging me to pursue this project. A special thanks to our research associate Katrina Bushko for helping this book along at each and every stage—from our very early efforts to track down interview subjects to the final details of the manuscript. You have, over the course of this project, been our constant saving grace.

To our former editor, Kate Gagnon, thank you for taking a chance on our idea.

To the entrepreneurs and thought leaders we spoke to over the past four years: your work is the real work. You have all left a lasting impression. There are too many to name, but in particular we're grateful to Sabari Raja, Eric Davis, Eric Wilson, Andrew Frishman, David Shapiro, Josh Schachter,

Mary Walsh, Joan Wasser-Gish, Gunnar Counselman, Chris Sturgis, Scott Van Beck, and Alexandra Bernadotte.

To Clay Christensen: thank you for your theories, your incredible mind, and your friendship. This book stands on your giant shoulders and your willingness to always ask why.

To my mentors: without you I would surely be even more unmoored than I already am. Gigi Bailey Bowden, you helped me find creativity by teaching me how to sew together new patches and recipes at every turn. John Faggi, you helped me find my writer within by patiently editing my incoherent prose. Renuka Kher, you help me find my inner compass by leading the way. Claire Este-McDonald, you help me find my intuition by scaffolding words and movement. Michael Horn, you help me find my voice by selflessly letting me borrow yours. Mom, Dad, and Rebecca, you help me—in spite of my early efforts to reject it—find delight in wrestling with thorny questions, engaging in dinner table debates, and cultivating the patience to learn.

And finally, to Daniel: but for you, this book would not have come about. So much of what we wrote about is that our opportunities spring forth from those we are lucky enough to meet. From chance encounters to deep collaborations, from brief flashes of inspiration in strangers' stories to enduring friendships and shared stories. We have, at different times over nearly two decades, spanned all of those. I am so blessed to know you.

Julia Freeland Fisher

I am a reluctantly social person, yet relationships seem always to have shaped the most meaningful periods of my life. Thanks to Mom and Dad for setting the bar high and for making me curious. Thanks to my sister, Katie, for always being there. You are my rock.

I joined the US Army not really knowing anyone in it. I came out of it with lifelong friendships. Thanks to Chris Mercado for your relentless wisdom and guidance. Thanks to my fellow officers for making me a better leader. Thanks to my NCOs for keeping me in check—whatever successes we had belong to you. Thanks to my soldiers for your tirelessness, enthusiasm, and humor. I love you all.

But mostly, of course, I want to thank Julia. Whom you know matters, but so does what you know about those who surround you. There's an understandable tendency in all of us to believe that our familiarity with others is asymptotic with time. We assume that the longer we've known someone, the less there is to discover. How wrong that assumption can be. You are even more remarkable than I imagined.

Daniel Fisher

INDEX

Page references followed by *fig* indicate an illustrated figure.